Reviews

Doctors' wordswordswords can become swordswordswords and kill or cure just like a scalpel can. We need to be trained to care for a person's life and experience and not just their diagnosis. If I had to write the foreword for Unspoken Messages you would think you were reading the same book twice. Richard and I have lived the experience with animals and life and death. He teaches and reveals to the reader the truths about consciousness, animal communication and more. For me the essential message is that just as a graduation is called a commencement and not a termination so is death. Like Richard I know what music I want played and the stories I want to hear at my funeral so I can die as my Dad did; looking great and laughing. But more importantly what the book relates are the lessons we need to learn about living in the time of our lives. Richard is what I call a survivor and his words can teach us to be survivors too. He is a wounded healer, ready to serve.

Bernie Siegel, MD author of Faith, Hope and Healing
and A Book of Miracles

You will find "Unspoken Messages" by Richard Rowland both an inspirational and delightful read. The spiritual lessons Richard shares are indeed messages to all. In each there is a distinct veracity that typically goes unspoken and unnoticed. I am convinced that all of us live lives full of special messages, or what has been called God winks, the uncanny coincidences that really aren't coincidences at all. You will find the winks are extraordinary in "Unspoken Messages" and they are guaranteed to lift your spirits and charm your being, sometimes by pulling a tear and sometimes by infusing joy! I urge you to read "Unspoken Messages."

Eldon Taylor, Ph.D., FAPA
NY Times Bestselling Author of Choices and Illusions

In his new book, **Unspoken Messages—Spiritual Lessons I learned from Horses and Other Earthbound Souls,** author, **Richard Rowland** exposes himself as a one-time, very cock-sure, and opinionated man, who becomes grounded by dark tragedies that light his way to a new mental path. He then inspires the reader with his newborn self—shifting into a high-realmed critical thinking that ranges from the flat board throes of earthly thoughts, all the way to a transcendental enlightenment. The author graciously points us toward these lessons that he has received from a place that few humans tread—his own soul. This story will take you to your knees with pain, and yet raise you up apart from the Earth, until you salute—not only the author, but your inner self! Where, "X" marks the spot, the reader will extrapolate that we all, who have breathed air are dying . . . and that death is simply a continuing, in the *Circle of Life*.

Richard Rowland literally unveils the philosophy of Plato, ". . . as a sensible man will remember that the eyes may be confused in two ways—by a change from light to darkness—or, from darkness to light; and he will recognize that the same thing happens to the soul".

Review by: Jim Hodges

Jim Hodges is an international public speaker, and author of a myriad of classified publications for intelligence, law enforcement, and the military. In a life parallel to his tactical roles, Jim has been a life-long cowboy, and horse trainer, and accomplished extensive work in national and international television, film, and video. Please check Jim's website at: www.cowboyspeaks.com for bookings.

UNSPOKEN MESSAGES

*Spiritual Lessons I Learned from Horses
and Other Earthbound Souls*

Sunrise signals the start of a new day. Copyright 2012 Richard D. Rowland

RICHARD D. ROWLAND

BALBOA.
PRESS
A DIVISION OF HAY HOUSE

Balboa Press books may be ordered through booksellers or by contacting:

Balboa Press
A Division of Hay House
1663 Liberty Drive
Bloomington, IN 47403
www.balboapress.com
1 (877) 407-4847

Because of the dynamic nature of the Internet, any web addresses or links contained in
this book may have changed since publication and may no longer be valid. The views
expressed in this work are solely those of the author and do not necessarily reflect the
views of the publisher, and the publisher hereby disclaims any responsibility for them.

The author of this book does not dispense medical advice or prescribe the use of any
technique as a form of treatment for physical, emotional, or medical problems without the
advice of a physician, either directly or indirectly. The intent of the author is only to offer
information of a general nature to help you in your quest for emotional and spiritual well-
being. In the event you use any of the information in this book for yourself, which is your
constitutional right, the author and the publisher assume no responsibility for your actions.

Any people depicted in stock imagery provided by Thinkstock are models,
and such images are being used for illustrative purposes only.
Certain stock imagery © Thinkstock.

Printed in the United States of America.

ISBN: 978-1-4525-8425-6 (sc)
ISBN: 978-1-4525-8427-0 (hc)
ISBN: 978-1-4525-8426-3 (e)

Library of Congress Control Number: 2013918402

Balboa Press rev. date: 11/19/2013

Dedicated

to

My wife, Jennifer, and

son, Richard.

Without their continuing love and support,

this endeavor may very well

have remained

merely a thought.

Contents

Acknowledgements...ix

Introduction..xiii

Part One **Let the Journey Begin**

Chapter One   And They All Said Good-bye..............................3

Chapter Two   Fixing a Broken Circle...................................13

Chapter Three Addio Nocciolina..27

Chapter Four   The Nature of Things 36

Chapter Five   The Circle Is Complete................................ 44

Chapter Six   An Unexpected Smile....................................54

Chapter Seven Wild-Eyed and Laid Up 61

Chapter Eight The Effects of Choice 71

Chapter Nine   Cookie and the Coon...................................99

Chapter Ten   Old Kate 111

Part Two **Coming Clean and Facing Fear**

Chapter One   Mind-Numbing News....................................127

Chapter Two   An Awakening..134

Chapter Three The Proof Is in the Evidence............................143

Chapter Four   Bumps in the Road to Recovery 154

Chapter Five   The Limitations of Allopathic Medicine
               and the Effect of Environmental Issues..............162

Chapter Six   When the Conclusion Isn't the End....................171

Chapter Seven Lessons I Have Learned....................................189

Suggested Reading List 203

References 205

Acknowledgements

When I first started this project I had no idea how much help I was going to need, nor did I realize how much time would be required of me and a great many people around me. Now that the process is winding down, it is time to thank those who made it happen.

First on the long list is my family; wife Jennifer and son Richard M. without whose love, understanding and support, this book would never have been written. There were countless hours where their only view of me was from the back as I sat in front of a computer, typing. Thank you both for helping me find the time to make this a reality. I will be back as a contributing member of this family unit soon.

Much appreciation is due to the many animals in my life, both living and passed who contributed to the subject matter of this book. I thank you for teaching me about the expansiveness of this world we live in and the message of ever present hope and spirits that live without end.

I view the rest of the acknowledgements in chronological order and forgive me if I leave anyone out. You have to remember, this has been an endeavor that started with a simple short story and lasted almost three years. I am staring at the finish line with a mind clouded by excitement.

First off, thank you to the many friends and co-workers who read my initial work and encouraged me to write a book. The journey began when you believed in and inspired me to continue touching people emotionally with words. You paved the road I traveled.

I am indebted to Sheila Jolly, a lady I went to school with many years ago who after reading some of my early work, introduced me to the publishing world via her friendship with Brenda Roberts. Brenda has been steadfast in her support and free with her advice and further introductions into a world I knew little about.

Sheila, Jimmy and Katie Puckett are due much gratitude for their assistance and insight into life with a horse I shared a previous experience with. They also spent hours on the phone with me, wrote many emails and provided pictures in order to give life to a story that needed to be told.

I am grateful for meeting and getting a chance to work with Richard Small, a talented photographer and the owner of Richard Small Photography in Ellsworth, Maine. I relayed to him what I wanted to capture in a photograph and he found the emotions I desired in the perfect picture to go with a story.

I have been blessed in life to have met and made friends with several artists, three of whom contributed to this project. Ann Clark Chambers and I attended school together and she graciously agreed to create a drawing based upon a thought, one that conveys a journey into the unknown. Another artist and friend is Agatha Kacprzak from Canada. She created a drawing from an out of focus picture and gave it life and emotion. Lastly, thanks to Jess Parker-Andrews from the UK, who also looked at a blurry picture and created a work of art as humorous as the situation depicted in the story.

Many thanks and much gratitude to Gregory R. Ambrose, the artist, designer who managed to tell a story with the cover of this book. The hours spent showcased his talent and depict a journey within and travels to the unknown.

My editors had a hard job to do and did it well. I have been schooled on the English language after finding out I didn't know what I thought I knew. Thanks Jeanne V. Benedict for getting me through the initial hurdles and the editorial staff at Balboa Press for the great line edit. I learned my lessons.

Adriane Pontecorvo, my coordinator from Balboa Press who has been my constant go-to person. Thank you for direction when I needed it and being my unceasing motivator. You never failed to have the answer and for that I sincerely thank you.

I genuinely appreciate my publisher, Balboa Press for believing in me and the message this book brings to those in need of hope. Without your faith in me the message might not have reached those in need of reading it.

Finally, thanks to Dr. Bernie Siegel, Dr. Eldon Taylor and Mr. Jim Hodges, authors who believed I had a message worth hearing. They are all tremendously gifted people capable of instilling hope where hope was stolen. I appreciate your time, encouragement and willingness to write reviews for this work.

©2013 A Chambers

Introduction

O NLY A VERY FEW YEARS ago, I was a much different man than the one I am today. I will admit, and most who know me would agree, I was hardheaded, opinionated, absolutely sure of my place in this world, and convinced that a science-based ideology was the only true ideology. I lived in a world of my own creation and belief where things were black or they were white; they were right or they were wrong; and they were proven or they did not exist. Nothingness is all that resided between the two conflicting areas. There were not any gray areas, and there were no what-ifs at all. I say "of my own creation," but upon reflection, these were the beliefs that I had been spoon-fed and had accepted without question during my formative years that created the person I became. I will admit, for most of my life, I was comfortable with the belief system I had cultivated.

I am not sure I was ever completely satisfied with my personality and enjoyed it, or if I simply acted the way I did because other people seemed to be comfortable with my persona. If I wasn't already a curmudgeon, I was certainly studying to be one and passing each test with flying colors. I was also a person who never entertained one single thought about the possibility of writing a book. It is sometimes thought provoking to look back and see how challenges that arise in our lives create an opportunity for real growth when you face them. The challenges I faced will be discussed in depth in part two of this book; the growth will be evident as I tell the tales of magic and unexplainable experiences throughout the entire book.

I grew up a child of the fifties, not much differently than other children of that era. We lived in a rural farming community named Elizabethtown, about an hour's drive from Louisville, Kentucky. I, as well as the great majority of my peers, was a child of war veterans, part of the famous baby boom. World War II had ended, the Korean War was beginning, and Vietnam was an unknown blip on the map. Science was making grand strides in discovery and not just with the atomic bomb. Western medicine and prescription drugs were becoming a mainstay for every illness imaginable, and people wanted a pill to fix everything.

At the same time, spirituality lost favor. Keep in mind that when I write of spirituality, I am not writing about religiosity. Although related, they are not exactly the same. Around this time, people's trust shifted from one belief to another. The end result was that science dazzled the masses, and your grandmother's natural treatment lost its favorite spot in the family's list of cure-alls. It is not that Granny's cure didn't work; it just lost its luster when science would not take the time to prove it worked and chose to promote pills instead. Prayer, faith, and belief, along with natural medicine, good, healthy food, holistic treatments, herbal cures, and other older medical mainstay cures took a back seat to the powerful engine running modern medicine. Thankfully, all of these things were not forgotten just because they lost favor. They remained hidden, waiting their turn to cycle back once again. You see, science and spirituality have knocked heads and exchanged places repeatedly for a long time.

About the time of the forced rebirth of my personal spirituality, thoughts of writing this book began to surface. I say a forced rebirth because if not for an illness that befell me, I am sure I would have continued to muddle through life just as I had been doing and would have missed out on experiencing a most wondrous opportunity for inner growth, which changed my whole life. When you look at the area where I grew up, it is smack in the middle of the Bible Belt. However, my family was not very religious. We never even made it to being considered

Christmas and Easter Christians. Our attendance at church, besides a couple of vacation Bible schools, was sporadic at best and usually occurred only when there was serious trouble brewing at home.

Life was full of trouble when you grew up in a house with three brothers. Early on, the whole family experienced its fair share of dysfunction. However, it rarely got to the point of having to ask God to intercede on our behalf, or so our parents believed. Nightly prayers were not something insisted upon or taught, so it should come as no surprise that my exposure to religious beliefs and spirituality was very lacking during my youth. Regardless of what many may believe to be a failure on the part of my parents, my siblings and I turned out just fine, even by today's standards.

The following work of non-fiction is split into two related parts. Part One is a collection of separate stories relating instances that I have witnessed over the past five years or instances from years past that I have revisited while armed with the new beliefs I hold dear. With one exception, the stories in Part One revolve around animals, mostly horses. A good number of the stories end up being tug-at-the-heartstrings types of tales, though a couple of them are humorous in nature.

Every story in Part One is spiritual in nature, and each contains a message to be conveyed to the reader. Some of the stories are intensely magical, bordering upon unbelievable to those not versed in spirituality, and may cause you to question my truthfulness. But I can assure you each of the stories in Part One are completely factual, and most were witnessed by people other than myself. In some of the stories, I have changed the names of the people or their cities of residence to protect their privacy. In other chapters, the real names and locations are used with permission. One of the stories, "And They All Said Goodbye," concerns an incident witnessed by many other people as well as myself, and it still stands as one of the most spiritual experiences I have ever been witness to—so far.

Part Two of this endeavor is a synopsis of a five-year plus period of my life from August 2008 through 2013. It will reveal to you the journey I made that brought about a major change in my life. I share how I changed from being the hardheaded person I was into the very spiritual, caring, compassionate, and believing person I am today.

As you journey through time with me, it may often seem as though I am attacking the practice of medicine in America. This is not completely the case. If you read until the end, you will see how important I believe balance is in our daily lives. You will also discover why I believe faith is the most important factor in the healing process. When writing about faith, I do so in the context of faith in the healing modality that you choose, without giving preference to any certain one. At no point in this book do I pretend to be a doctor of any kind, nor have I been schooled in medicine or research. I do not hold completely negative views of doctors, only the particular doctors I took issue with based on personal experiences concerning my health and longevity. The views I write about are mostly mine, but some are from those like-minded individuals I surround myself with, who shared with me while discussing the state of modern Western medicine.

Please do not think I am giving you medical advice. I am not. I am merely telling you what worked for me and worked for me well, from the moment in time I was misled into believing hope was dead until this very day. Hope is something that should never be taken from you by anyone, especially those you are paying to treat you medically. Hope should always be balanced by possibilities and delivered in that manner. Doctors should not deliver a diagnosis based upon the unfeeling, uncaring, statistical data that they allow themselves to be spoon-fed and then orally regurgitate. Their patients are the people for whom they are supposed to be life's stewards. Miracles happen every day, and if miracles can happen for one person, they are possible for all people. Search for the way to make yours come true.

Now, join me on this journey of possibilities.

RDR

Part One

LET THE JOURNEY BEGIN

The road ahead, copyright Jennifer Benedict
Rowland/ Double R Stables Kentucky

Chapter One

And They All Said Good-bye

For every good-bye, God also provides a hello.
—Donna Gable Hatch

THIS IS A STORY ABOUT the tragic death of one of the best horses I have ever had the honor to share ground with. Sadly, I also shared her last hour. It was one of the worst days I have had with horses, but it was also one of the most amazing spiritual experiences I have ever had.

Her registered name was "Buff and Fancy," but we called her Buffy. She was a big-boned girl; she had a pretty sorrel coat and an intelligent, soft eye. I often described her as so light to pressure that you didn't have to do much more than think what you wanted her to do and she would already be doing it. When handling or riding horses, you communicate through cue and release signals. The cue comes from pressure of some kind, and the release is the end of the pressure. If you want to lead a horse, you put slight pressure on the lead rope until the horse gives to the pressure and starts to move forward. As soon as the horse moves in the direction you want, you release the pressure or stop pulling and let the horse walk.

Saying Buffy was light to pressure is actually an understatement. It took very little to get her to comply with what I wanted her to do. It didn't matter what deed we had to accomplish, she would do it willingly. She also had the uncanny ability to sense just how knowledgeable you were when working with her. If she sensed you didn't have much experience, she would take advantage of the situation—not in a way that would hurt someone, but she would develop an uncooperative attitude. I witnessed this in her interaction with others but never with me. I have never experienced such good ground manners in any horse before or since. To top it off, she was a super mom. The little filly foal by her side on this hot late-July day had been born on May 12, 2009, at 1:20 a.m. I know because I shared that hour with her as well.

Almost all of the foals born in my presence were born in the middle of the night, generally between 1:00 and 5:00 a.m. I don't know why this is the rule, but it certainly seems to be. I can only remember one foal that was born during daylight hours. When Buffy gave birth to her little filly, I was spending the night in the barn foaling horses. I wanted to be present for many reasons. The potential of a medical problem was at the top of the list, but imprinting was a close second. My goal has been to imprint a foal when it is born and to be with it from the start if at all possible. I want the foal to smell my presence as soon as the birth sack opens. Then I leave it to bond with his or her mother.

That night, I had a couple of mares that were really close to foaling and, as always, I made it my practice to be there when it happened. Too many things can go wrong during a birth, and you do not want to lose either the mare or the foal. I have lost count of the number of nights I slept fitfully in the barn awaiting nature's magic, but I never tired of doing my part.

Some mares will not have a foal in your presence. They will cross their legs, so to speak, and refuse to start the process. They spend their time looking serenely about in the foaling stall as if it were just another day on the farm. Those horses wait until you go to the house for a cup of coffee and have the foal while you are gone, even if you are absent for only ten minutes. Then there are those like Annie, another of our horses. She would actually wake me up if I had managed to fall asleep. She would stick her head over the stall wall, gently grab my shoulder with her lips, and give me a wake-up shake when it was time. Annie knew she always needed a little help, and she wanted me there.

I had never foaled Buffy before, so I didn't know how she would behave. As it turned out, she was one of those mares that actually wanted me to be present. She didn't have to wake me up because I started seeing the signs around midnight that foaling was imminent. She started pacing, sweat patches started appearing on her chest, and she was shaking her head and backing up against the stall wall. All of these are signs that the show is about to begin. At 1:20 a.m., with a little help from me pulling during contractions, her big but healthy filly was born. After I opened the birth sack and blew a little air toward the foal's face, I left Buffy to do her part. I went back to being an observer of nature at its best.

Sam Owsley of Massachusetts was Buffy's owner. Over the years, we have kept several of Sam's horses, mostly brood mares sent to Double R Stables to have babies. Little did we know that this little filly foaled by Buffy and affectionately called Peanut, would be her last offspring. I have often thanked Sam for sending Buffy here to share time with us. I have also apologized for having to call him with such bad news and for the heavy decision that he had to make without being here. Bad situations often create a bond between those who experience them. This one did just that.

Buffy's foal was the last one to be born at the stables. In addition, the health challenges I had been facing for the year prior to that night made it too taxing for me to keep up with the demands this type of endeavor required of me. My time spending nights in the barn from late January until April of each year was over. I miss the magic of being involved so deeply with nature, but I really do not miss the dusty cold barn.

It was late in the afternoon on a normally hot summer day in Kentucky. Buffy was spending time in the barn lot with her filly. The barn lot is a relatively small area. It's fenced off from the pastures, and animals housed there have access to the back of the barn and the stalls for getting out of the sun or inclement weather as needed. Even though small, the barn lot allows horses staying in it to visit with and touch noses with other horses living in pastures. Buffy never missed a chance to visit and be sociable prior to her foal being born and seemed to get along with all the other horses. The need to be in a herd setting was apparent. Things changed after Peanut was born and she became more protective.

Also located in the barn lot is a structure called a round pen. Round pens are corral-like structures. They resemble farm gates that are used to close off areas. They are fifteen feet long by five feet high and have metal fingers on the vertical ends that interlock with other panels. This interlock accepts a metal, hooked pin that holds the panels in place and allows you to build any configuration you desire. The fingers are a loop of metal about six inches long and about an inch wide. Round pens are normally sixty feet in diameter when used for training horses, but they can be used for small pens, squares, or rectangles. Buffy was enjoying being a mother and biding her time in this area until Peanut was ready to experience the fields and respect the high tensile fences that surrounded them.

Buffy and her foal, Peanut. Copyright © 2009 Richard D. Rowland

I was in the house when I received a phone call from Lee Graves who was out near the pen. He told me young Peanut had started running toward the round pen which was occupied by a gelding. Buffy, being one who never much cared for her filly being around the gelding took off at a gallop and placed herself between Peanut and him. Lee said Buffy was actually rubbing herself against the round pen panels as she ran, determined to keep her body between Peanut and the other horse.

Peanut with the round pen in the background.
Copyright © 2009 Richard D. Rowland

Somehow, Buffy hooked one of the round pen panel fingers with her hip. The force drove the metal into her side, struck and broke her pelvis, and pulled part of the bone out. She hit with such force that she caused the panels to accordion together; one of the panels was almost bent double. She knew immediately that she was in trouble.

According to Lee, she walked a few steps, stared at the house, and waited for me. I was always the one to come if she needed someone, which certainly wasn't often. In fact, the only other time I was ever needed was to help deliver her foal. Looking back, I believe the bond between us became unbreakable that night when new life arrived and brought magic with it.

After Lee had finished telling me what had happened, I left the house and headed to the barn lot, feeling nervous and worried. Even though he explained clearly on the phone what had occurred, I still had trouble picturing how things could possibly be as bad as he indicated. When I arrived, Buffy stood still and looked at me with her soft brown eyes as I checked her over.

I am sure that my eyes confirmed what she already knew: this was a bad situation. My wife, Jennifer, was with me, and I was unable to meet her gaze, even though I could feel it. Our son, Matt, watched as well. I put one hand on Buffy's shoulder, feeling the familiar warmth and comfort that always came when I was around this amazing horse. I was hoping she could read my heart and the love I felt, but not the fear. Although only eleven years old, if there ever was an old soul in a horse body, she was an example of it. My other hand went to my cell phone.

I called the local large animal veterinarian service as soon as I had assessed the injury. It was still bright daylight but after hours. I reached Dr. Michael Thomas at home. The good thing about the services I use is that if you call after hours, the phone rings at one of the partner's homes. They know me and know I will not call unless it is a dire emergency that I cannot address. Mike and I have been friends for years, and he had made several trips to the stables in the past. I guess he could tell from the tone of my voice that he was needed badly.

I put a rope halter on Buffy even though I didn't need it. Still fearful and in pain, she stood with me and waited. She did lie down briefly a time or two, but mostly we just stood together with my hand on her shoulder or stroking her neck. I talked to her softly and reassuringly, and she stood, apparently listening as most horses will, to the cadence and tone of my voice. Never once did she complain or try to walk away.

Her breathing remained steady, and her gaze on her foal or me never wavered. She even allowed her foal to nurse as often as she needed.

While I was waiting for Mike, I made another phone call. I called Sam with the bad news and told him I would call back as soon as I had more information. It was a difficult call to make. I had to describe what had occurred and how bad I thought the injury to her pelvis was, but I tried to remain calm during the conversation. I kept my hand on the mare's shoulder for comfort and kept my eyes constantly on hers so that no one could tell I was screaming inside at the injustice I felt.

Thankfully, it didn't take Mike long to arrive. He did an in-depth examination of the wound, which included having to insert his fingers into it in order to check the pelvic area. Silently, Buffy stood with me, never once shying away or flinching from the intrusion. He confirmed what I already knew. This was a bad situation, and little could be done. Her pelvis was badly broken, and she had a lot of soft tissue damage. A drain could be inserted and the area stitched up, but with the severity of the damage, it would only prolong the inevitable. His advice was to put her out of her current and coming misery. It's funny, even though all along I knew this would probably be the outcome, part of me had held out for a miracle. I wanted what I wanted and did not want to allow the world to work the way it was meant to. What the mare and I shared now went much deeper than anything we ever envisioned when we first met.

It was now time for another phone call, the last one of the night. I called Sam once more, and we had a lengthy conversation this time. As hard as it was to report the news and give the advice, I know it was harder for him to actually make the decision he was faced with making. He conferred with Mike, listened to his assessment, and the choice was made. We had to let Buffy go.

You can say what you want to about animals, but I have spent a lifetime with them. I know they have feelings. I know they have a soul, and I know they are intuitive. I never knew their level of intuition

9

until that night. I believe with all my being that Buffy knew and felt the energy change around us. I believe she realized what was about to happen, and when she realized it she laid down. Her eyes once again went to mine ever so briefly, as if to tell me she knew and she understood her time in this physical world was coming to an end. Then she called to Peanut, and in that soft murmuring sound mares only make to their foals, she apparently said her good-byes. I listened to the soft sounds coming from deep within her, and I watched the look of puzzlement on Peanut's face. I know I witnessed the communication between these two animals; I saw it and heard it. I came to believe later that she said much more than good-bye.

Mike asked if I could get the foal into the round pen, so I put the gelding in his stall and opened one of the panels outward. I separated Peanut from her mother, who remained lying on the ground, and put her in the round pen with surprising ease. Normally, herding foals is like herding cats; it just cannot be easily done until they have been trained a little. Peanut minded as if she knew exactly what I wanted of her. This was the first of many surprises this little filly had in store for me. Whatever passed between the two of them stuck with Peanut, and she went forward wiser than she had begun the night. By this time, darkness had closed around us and brought with it the power of the universe in order to teach us something of a world we knew little about.

Mike administered the series of shots that are used to put large animals to sleep. At that exact moment in time, in complete darkness, seemingly timed with the injection of the first shot, nineteen other horses located in various lots around the acres that encompass the stables started nickering, whinnying, and running like crazy. Most of these horses could not see what was going on, but they all knew. And one horse did not start it; they all started at exactly the same time. Horses were raring, pawing the air, kicking up a dust storm, running as fast as they could and calling out loudly over and over.

The hair stood up on my arms and neck as I witnessed all that was going on around me. After a few minutes, Buffy faded away, and the din died down. It died down just as it started—all at once. We went from the original complete quiet as we talked and decided Buffy's fate to the display as described above and then back to complete silence. It was as if someone had their hand on a control switch and could turn the volume on and off, the change was that quick. After Buffy died, the other horses went back to what horses do without a glance in our direction.

All of the five people present looked at each other in amazement and realized that we had been part of something special. We had been given a glimpse of the magic that exists every day just outside our senses. A friend later described it as a "God wink," and I found myself in agreement. It turned out to be a final gift from Buffy and a lesson in the nature of things from the other horses. All the horses knew what was transpiring and gave their send off and well wishes. How did they know? I think the circle of energy they are part of allows them to feel more than we realize, and science doesn't have an answer for that. Horses know more than we think. They are smarter than we can imagine. All animals have this gift, and I firmly believe that you do too; just search it out and you will find it. I did, and I have witnessed and experienced enough to know there is much more out there than most people believe possible.

Through this experience and a few others during the past five years or so, I have come to the realization we are all part of a single energy. Call it what you wish, but in my mind it exists. We are all part of God. We are all together on this living planet. Our energies intermingle with all the others. Let's take a lesson from this tragedy and the actions of these amazing animals. There is so much more to this existence than most of us ever thought possible. Open your eyes to the shades of gray. For much of my life, I saw things in black and white. Don't be like I was. See like I do now. Amazing possibilities exist and are waiting for you to experience them.

I went out the next morning and spent some time with Buffy. While her offspring watched from the pen, I stroked her neck, head, and shoulder and realized how sorely I already missed the warmth of her being and the soft gaze of her brown eyes. I wanted so badly for her to get up and be what I remembered: a friend to talk to when no one else was around and a steadying presence after a trying day. I missed the closeness we shared, that we all share with animals who we have stewardship over and responsibility for. I realized the gift she left me with, but I still wanted her companionship back. I wanted *her* to teach her foal about being a horse, not me. In the end, I thanked her for the time we shared together and the look into the other side that she had given me. I promised to do the best I could by her foal, Peanut. I said my goodbyes and went about my day as I always do, one step forward at a time and a believer in the mystery of the unknown.

Chapter Two

Fixing a Broken Circle

Until one has loved an animal, a part of
one's soul remains unawakened.
—Anatole France

RUNNING A FARM OR AN equine agriculture business is like
standing inside a circle of many intricate parts that all have to
work in conjunction with each other in order to make the endeavor
succeed. We are in the process of putting the circle back together after
two of our farm animals crossed over the rainbow bridge. For those
readers unfamiliar with the concept of the rainbow bridge, it is written
that a bridge exists where animals' souls cross over when they die.
There, they are provided with all they need and are restored to good
health. As their owners make the transition after their own passing,
they are reunited with their beloved pets and companions. I do so
love the story of the rainbow bridge, especially in light of the fact that
our hard-working and devoted barn cat, Whiskers, and our cherished
golden retriever, Sarge, crossed that bridge within a week of each other.
The idea of seeing the two of them, as well as all of the other treasured
animals that preceded me in death, intrigues me and fills my soul with
hope for a grand reunion.

Whiskers the barn cat was eleven and had been a fixture on the
farm since he was five weeks old. When he was younger, he was quite

adventurous and was once seen sitting on top of the electric pole next to the barn trying to catch birds. He managed to make it down by himself after I informed him that I was not going to call the fire department. He was also quite a mouser for many years, but eventually he became bored of the many available mice around the barns and could be seen at times simply watching them as they scurried around the barn in search of morsels of feed instead of giving chase, as most cats would. He elected instead to come to the house and catch songbirds at the feeders, perhaps from some need to have a prey fear his presence instead of mocking him. After his death, the mice reclaimed possession of the barn and the birds felt safe once again.

Whiskers

Whisker's arrival at our farm came after the disappearance of a buff-colored tomcat we had dubbed Drifter. Drifter showed up at our house shortly after we moved here. We never knew if Drifter was simply traveling through or if someone dropped him off, so the name seemed a good fit. Drifter was here one day and gone a few months later, after earning the love of a small boy. Faced with a missing member of our family, I went in search of a new cat to fill the void. The search started in our local newspaper, which was filled with "free to a good home" ads giving away kittens. I am not sure why one in particular caught my eye, but it did. After a phone call and a short trip, I was reunited with a former classmate from high school who had a litter of five kittens to give away.

All of the visible kittens looked the same: little puffs of dark-gray fur with bright eyes. Seeing only four kittens, I asked her where the fifth kitten was. She told me I probably wouldn't want him, since he was the runt of the litter and not very sociable. I must say that the possibility of taking a kitten who no one else would want fit the needs of my heart at the time, and I asked to see him. She found him behind the couch and brought the shy little fella out. My decision was made. This would be the kitten I would take home with me. I liked his independent nature and wouldn't have wanted him to be anything more than he was. Part of him wanted to be around you, but he never begged for attention. It seemed like he viewed our relationship as a partnership. I guess you could say he won me over from the very beginning. I wasn't a lap-cat-type person, and he wasn't a lap-cat-type feline.

So many stories could be told about this dedicated family member that I have to hope he forgives me for only writing of the highlights instead of dedicating a whole book to his escapades. I still remember bringing Whiskers home from the veterinarian after having him fixed the summer of his first year. My hope was to keep him from wandering, as tomcats are apt to do, and I thought this would solve the problem. On the way home, he wanted to get under my feet as I drove the pick-up truck. I kept making him move, and he kept coming back. After one rather forceful removal from under the gas pedal, he looked at me with a defiantly angry glare. He promptly moved to the other side of the truck and sprayed the floor. Those who have had the misfortune to smell cat spray know what I went through. It is not as bad as a skunk but still quite odorous. I don't think the smell ever completely left that truck.

Whiskers was a very independent cat his whole life and a much-loved member of our farm family. He never turned into a lap cat, since it was one of those things he never aspired to, but he got along with everyone here, including his buddy Sarge. He even got along with another cat we introduced him to.

We didn't have a goal of having another barn cat, but sometimes fate intervenes and things change. Jennifer worked in town for a little while, and she came home one day and told a story about a poor cat with a ragged ear that was hanging around her place of employment. She said people were feeding the cat from their leftover lunches, and he was eating anything they would give him, including green beans and mashed potatoes. She asked if she could bring him home and nurse him back to health. After discussing the matter for all of one minute, the decision was made to try to catch the cat and see if we could help him back to health. She took a pet carrier to work and returned that afternoon with a gray tabby cat that had a ragged right ear and definitely needed some tenderness in his life.

Now, here is a funny twist if there ever was one. A year before Jennifer rescued this cat, a friend gave me a cat for the barn because he was moving and couldn't take him. He was a gray tabby cat with a little white on his chest, a ragged right ear from a previous fight, and as a plus, he had been neutered and vaccinated. I brought him home and put him in the tack room of the barn for two days to acclimate him to his new home. The day I decided to open the tack room and let our recent addition explore his new home, he promptly ran directly out of the barn, never once looked back, and never returned. Or did he? I could swear this new cat we named Hobo was one and the same. He had the same white chest and ragged ear as the cat that escaped long ago, and he too was neutered. If it was in fact the same cat, I have to wonder what went through his mind when he was returned to the place he had escaped from the year before. Life is without doubt cyclic. Hobo lived with us for two years before succumbing to feline leukemia. Whiskers and Hobo had become good friends while ruling the barn together during those two years, and it was very apparent in his actions and demeanor that Whiskers missed his friend.

When Whiskers crossed the rainbow bridge, he died alone in a stall of the barn that had been his castle. From all appearances, he lay down to sleep and never chased another mouse or worried another bird, at least in this universe. He was buried in the side yard to the south of the house under the limbs of a tall pine tree. It was the same place where he used to love to hunt birds or lay in deep sleep, perhaps lulled to slumber by the wind whispering through the pines ever so softly. We hope he found another pine tree to rest under after crossing over, a peaceful place in which to patiently await our reunion.

I don't think it matters how many holes you dig in the yard or around the farm in order to bury beloved pets; they all represent an individual set of loving memories, filed away for a time only to be revisited fondly long after they pass. We will always have room for more holes and many more memories. We will always welcome the opportunity to share our time on this earth interacting with and learning from the wonderful ageless souls that reside within the hearts of animals everywhere.

≈

Sarge was another large part of our family during his eleven years, and also a loyal and trusted companion. He was an extremely smart dog with a good command of our spoken language. He didn't always follow our commands, but he did know what we wanted him to do. Sometimes he would look at you when you wanted him to do something, pause, and get a funny, faraway look in his eyes. You could imagine him saying, "Silly man, you don't really think I will mind you when I am so busy doing what I prefer. When I am finished with this matter at hand, I will come back to see you."

Sarge was a large-framed golden retriever. We found him through an advertisement, and even though he was located several miles away in Scottsville, Kentucky, we decided to take a day trip to look at him and his littermates. He was from a litter of fifteen puppies but he was the most sociable and lively of the bunch. He locked onto the smallest of our group, Matt, whom we called "the boy." In no time at all, they were playing together, and Sarge was enjoying having his belly tickled. I guess he picked us to go home with, and we couldn't help but agree.

Animals often play a part in picking their new homes. I once had a horse named Shiloh, a handsome four-year-old spotted appaloosa. I had ridden him a little, but I was in the process of buying the farm we now live on and I needed cash. At that time, I bought and sold horses, and I knew he was a good one I could easily sell. I eventually had three different people come to see and ride him, but he wouldn't do anything they wanted him to do. One person even called him "green broke at best," meaning he had a lot to learn. Well, I knew this horse was better than green broke. I had ridden him and had others ride him without any issues. Then one day a lady named Michelle came to see him. Michelle is the wife of a co-worker and someone I consider my friend. That day, Shiloh behaved like a perfect gentleman. He obeyed every cue, even did a little reining spin, and gave every impression of being the well-trained horse he was, thoroughly stealing Michelle's heart. She bought him, and they have been together some thirteen years now. Animals are very intuitive and in all probability more spiritually enlightened than we are. It is my fervent belief that old souls abound, and Shiloh is an old soul who picked the person he wanted to go home with and rejected the others.

Coming from such a large litter, Sarge felt he had to fight for his food. The first lesson he had to learn after we brought him home was not to bite, snarl, or fight at feeding time. He learned that lesson well, and within the first year he would not eat until he was told it was okay. Once given that okay, though, he would attack his food with gusto, devouring it seemingly without pausing to take a breath. Never once did he slow down to taste exactly what he was eating. He would sometimes eat without chewing and issue several loud burps when finished. I'm pretty sure that Sarge was the first dog I ever heard burp!

Sarge was a great varmint dog. He kept all kinds of animals away from the farm, including coyotes, foxes, possums, and skunks. A good varmint dog is an absolute necessity on any farm. Without him, these other animals rapidly multiply to become pests and take over in quick order. Like many dogs, however, Sarge had to learn his lesson about skunks the hard way.

We were used to hearing Sarge bark at night. His barking was generally in chorus with the coyotes howling in the distance. But one night, we heard the most ferocious barking and a deep, resonant growling coming through the windows. Thinking we had a prowler, I was in the process of getting up to check when the noise abruptly stopped. There was complete and utter silence. Initially, I was worried about Sarge's safety. I feared something or someone had dispatched old Sarge in order to ensure their successful completion of some dark deed. Isn't it funny where your mind travels in the middle of the night after an abrupt awakening?

About that time, it hit—the truly terrible, pungent odor of skunk spray. It filled the house! The odor was so strong that you could actually taste it. Everyone was up in an instant trying to close the windows against the onslaught of the musky stench. That's when we heard a faint but distinctive whimper. Old Sarge had received his first schooling about skunks, and that lesson was to give them a wide berth without fail.

Among Sarge's many skills was his ability to catch mice. He could shame most cats when it came to chasing and catching them. Sarge was an exceptional mouser, maybe even better than Whiskers, who was at this time semi-retired. You could call him, say the word "mouse," and point. He would find the mouse, catch it, and throw it in the air, and when it hit the ground, it would be dead. Then he would play with his prize for hours.

Sarge had all the delivery people and mail carriers trained to show up with dog treats. At times, he seemed to be a co-driver for various delivery people, especially those from United Parcel Service. As soon as they opened the door, he would be inside the truck begging for treats or a pat on the head. We often said that Sarge was not really a guard dog and would actually help you carry off anything you might want for the price of a dog treat. He loved attention and would die of starvation if someone continued to pet him long enough.

He had no idea how large he actually was and would even climb in your lap for attention if you didn't succeed in stopping him. There has never been a more loving dog. Part of this could be credited to the breeding of golden retrievers. Another part was the socialization we exposed him to during his first year of life, but the largest part was just his individual personality and spirit. Sarge truly cared about people. He could read your mind, an ability I believe all animals have. If you were down emotionally for some reason, he would sit quietly as you lightly stroked his massive head and contemplated your woes. If you felt playful, he would turn into a puppy, albeit a rather large one, and dart around with youthful enthusiasm.

There are so many stories I could tell about the relationship I had with this animal, but I will settle for sharing just one here. Sarge did me a wonderful favor one early winter day that eased a large burden on my heart. We had some square-baled hay on the ground next to the fence. We kept it covered with a tarp against the weather and would feed horses twice a day from that centrally located spot. I had to take my gloves off in order to open and use my knife to cut the baling string on a new bale of hay. When pulling the strings out from around the bale of hay, you use a rapid, jerking motion. I didn't realize it at the time I performed this oft repeated chore, but my wedding ring apparently flew off my finger to parts unknown. I had lost so much weight as a result of illness during the winter that I never felt it leave my hand. I did not discover the loss of my ring until much later in the day. It was the first time it had been off since Jennifer and I were married. I guess it had been on my finger so long that even though it was gone, it felt like it was still there.

Now I know a little about lost wedding rings, because my father lost his twice in his life. It makes me wonder if such a thing could be hereditary. Once, while working on a mower in the fall of one of my early childhood years, my father lost his wedding ring and apparently stepped on it in front of the barn, pushing it into the soft earth. Like me, he was devastated by the loss. He searched and searched to no avail; the ring just couldn't be found. We didn't have a lot of money when I was growing up, so replacing the ring was out of the question. The following spring, after the freezing, thawing, and ground heaving cycle was over, he saw a reflective glint on the ground and found the ring sitting atop the soil right where he had worked the previous fall.

Happy as he was to find the ring, he did manage to lose track of it one more time. Like me, he had also lost some weight as he aged and one spring, while working in the garden, he lost the ring again. Unable to find it, he was again saddened by the loss, but then, as unbelievable as it may seem, early that fall while harvesting carrots, he found his ring with a carrot growing right through the middle of it! From that point on, my father kept better track of his wedding ring, which I eventually inherited and still keep in a safe place.

At the time, it was quite an unusual story to tell, but as I have aged, I have come to believe in miracles and magic being common if you know how to harness your power. My father wanted desperately to find the ring and hoped to find it during harvest or while putting the garden to bed for the winter. He was convinced it would show up then and, strange as it is, that is exactly what happened. I don't believe it was a coincidence—I believe his confidence led to a miracle.

You would think that experiencing my father's lost rings firsthand would have taught me something, but I found myself exactly where he had been. Life seemingly cycles as such. I was evolving and I was learning about the new me and what was possible by being positive, but I wasn't quite as believing as I should have been. My faith went to science. After telling Jennifer and Matt about losing the ring and telling them where I thought I lost it, we began to search. We searched on hands and knees. We searched with a metal detector. We searched for days, which turned into weeks. We searched until I finally gave up any hope of finding my ring, and like my father, I was devastated.

When Sarge was little, I taught Matt how strong a canine sense of smell could be. We would take a small pebble, mark it with a little dot from a felt-tipped marker, and rub the pebble in our hands repeatedly until we were sure we had our scent on it. Then we would throw the rock in the middle of our gravel driveway with other like-sized rocks. Sarge always loved to fetch things, and he would go find the rock we threw and bring it back to us. Every time, he would bring back the pebble that we had marked. I am sure he smelled my scent on that ring and brought it back to me just as he had the pebbles long ago.

One afternoon, I was returning from the barn after my afternoon feeding chores. The barn is separated from the barn lot by a four-board fence and a walk-through gate. We have a path worn in the grass where we walk back and forth as we do many of the chores related to the horse business. At the house end of that path are the steps going up to the deck behind our house. On the first step lay my ring, still wet with dog drool, and on the top step sat Sarge with a contented look on his face. If he could only talk I am sure he would have said, "Look what I found! Throw it!" There was no doubt in my mind that he found the ring in the yard and laid it where I could see it. The ring smelled of dog. I bet he thought I had gone crazy the way I loved on him and told him what a good dog he was for finding my lost treasure. It would have been impossible to show Sarge the amount of gratitude I felt towards him for the gift he brought me. My heart was finally at ease.

In June of what was to be Sarge's last year, we noticed a slowing of his gait and a slight limp from his left front leg. He started spending more time in the shade and less time being the farm greeter, which is like being a Wal-Mart greeter only wetter. We knew something was going on with his health and had taken him to the veterinarian five times for shoulder pain. Several things were tried, but nothing worked. On a Monday, I returned with him one more time. They x-rayed him while he was lying on his back and discovered a large tumor on the inside of his shoulder. A biopsy indicated removal would solve the problem, and surgery was scheduled for Friday morning.

I took Sarge in the night before and let the assistant lead him off. I did not say a proper good-bye, just a "See you in the morning, buddy." He wagged his tail and walked off with the air of one who knows that wherever he is, he belongs. That was the last time I saw him alive. My friend never woke up from the surgery. It has at times bothered me that I did not say good-bye and maybe rough his ears a bit or pat his side. Then again, I realize it was probably better the way it happened. We took a leap of faith together and hoped all would be well.

The cancer was much too involved to be removed without also removing his front leg and shoulder. Sarge was too large at 120 pounds to ever recover from a major surgery like that, so the decision was made not to wake him from his sleep. Later that day, I went to the veterinarian's office to pick up Sarge's things. I hugged his body, petted him, and cried like an eight-year-old losing his first pet. This dog was my friend, and it would be difficult to get over the loss.

Growing up in rural Kentucky, animals were a large part of our existence. My favorite book during my formative years was a book by Fred Gipson titled *Old Yeller*. It was the first of many books that made me cry and set the stage for my future travels with the printed word. It became the genre of books that I was drawn to. If a book had an animal on the cover I would read it. I used to have a borrowed, dog-eared copy of *Old Yeller,* long ago returned to its owner but remembered fondly. Whether in life or print, experiences with animals crossing the rainbow bridge have the effect of imprinting part of their soul on yours; they never leave you completely, and memories of them will often come to mind. My feeling is that Sarge will be in my thoughts for a long time to come. Living on a farm can be a lonely existence at times. Your animals are companions and someone to talk to during times of solitude.

Sarge

Within a week of Sarge's passing, a fox was in the yard trying to get a chicken we were babysitting, and the rabbits wouldn't stay out of the gardens. They didn't wait long to take advantage of Sarge's absence. We loved our animals and missed them every day. But the time finally comes when you realize the openings they left in the circle have to be mended. Their ghosts remain part of the farm, but we needed replacements to do the work.

≈

You cannot have a farm and not have barn cats and a varmint dog, so we went to a no-kill shelter in Radcliff called Debbie's Rescue. Debbie had dozens of cats that desperately needed homes. They were all neutered or spayed and had their appropriate vaccinations. We adopted two cats, an eight-month-old male called Billy and a ten-month-old female who had been named Slick. Mistaken for a male at an early age, Slick is now named Grace for Grace Slick of Jefferson Airplane fame, because we wanted her to have a proper, gender-based name. Bill is a purring machine and Grace is regal. They quickly accepted the barn as their new home. The hunting began right away and soon they were giving us gifts of dead mice.

We added Debbie's Rescue to our monthly donation list. She has a wonderfully big heart, she has lots of animals to care for, and she receives little in the way of support. Most of the upkeep, feeding, vet bills, and the like come from her own pocketbook.

Grace and Billy

I went to the local animal control center a few times trying to find a dog that, if not adopted, would be destroyed. I think Sarge would have liked it that way, and I knew my heart would feel better if we could successfully adopt such a dog to fit our needs. Any dog we adopted would have to get along with the animals here; cats, horses, and whatever other animal in need that happened to capture our hearts. And it would have to pick up where Sarge left off keeping the varmints at bay and loving this family. I've no doubt we will find the right dog to bring home. Meanwhile, it seems the yard will continue to be dotted with the graves of past pets—graves which not only house the remains of our much loved pets but also a part of each member of this family who loved and cared for them. We keep every memory of their existence fresh in our minds and are constantly reminded of the wonderful times we shared.

The circle is partially repaired, and I have faith it will soon once again be complete. I am beginning to feel the power that I am sure will grow stronger in me as my journey of emotional healing continues. I miss Sarge and Whiskers every day, but as always, we must move forward. I feel sure this story will be continued as we move on down life's path toward the bridges we have yet to cross. Of that, I am confident and as always, I believe!

Chapter Three

Addio Nocciolina

The beginning is the most important part of the work.
—Plato

IT IS TIME TO CONTINUE the saga of the orphan filly affectionately known as Peanut. *Addio Nocciolina*, translated from Italian, means "Good-bye, Peanut." Peanut was not the orphaned filly's given name. I am not sure we ever knew her registered name, but we started referring to her as Peanut shortly after the death of her mother, Buffy. Most registered horses will be called a nickname related to their official moniker, but I can assure you that "Peanut" had nothing to do with her certified name and everything to do with her physical size. She was only six weeks old and was still a tiny thing.

The situation that made her an orphan touched all of us in a spiritual way and remains both a sad day in our memory and also a wondrous day in our enlightenment. We have moved on, as we all must, away from the emotional toll that day took, with our eyes open to the possibilities ahead. I guess, in a way, the journey with Buffy, Peanut, and I mirrored the path I was on. There are times in life when the only options are to move on or give up. Make the choice wisely, because the option you choose could very well set your emotional compass for any future decisions you make. Giving up becomes easier the more you do it.

Having spent a large part of my life around horses and surrounding myself with "horse people," I have a little bit of experience with the animals. I can say with confidence that orphaned horses, by and large, do not end up being good people horses. They are usually pushy, disrespectful, demanding animals that can't find their way with other horses or people. This is not their fault, because the seeds of possible failures are sown the moment they become orphaned. This is not to say that the reverse doesn't happen; it does. It is just rare for an orphan to turn out like Peanut did. The cards are usually stacked against them.

Foals turn out better, generally speaking, if their mothers raise them, introduce them to the herd, teach them horse politics, protect them, and discipline them. In many species, there are lessons which need to be taught by both parents, but in horses specifically, lessons are taught by the mother. Books have been written about the relationship between the dam and foal, and Peanut missed what these books teach us about what takes place during this transference of information. She went from being a loved and nurtured little foal to being alone in the world. She went from getting her nourishment from her mother to getting it from a bottle and supplements. She went from being part of an equine family to being by herself in a barn lot surrounded by people. Lastly, the love she received came from these strange things called humans and not from other horses. This is definitely far from the ideal situation in which a herd animal could mature and learn to coexist with others of its species.

Other horses usually shun orphans. It is said that they see them as a danger to the herd because they will attract predators. It certainly makes sense that other horses would not want a weaker member of the herd putting them at risk. Nature can seem hard sometimes, just as your life experiences may seem harsh to you.

Sometimes you can get a mare that has lost a foal to take an orphan or perhaps get a mare with a foal to nurse an orphan along with her own offspring. It is beautiful and heartwarming when it does happen, but it is rare and takes a special mare to allow it. We had neither set of circumstances available to us in this case, so it was the bottle, milk supplements, and a quick move to rations suited to a much older horse that we relied on to bring Peanut along.

She was needy and clingy at first, which was normal. As much as we loved the little horse being so friendly, we knew it could not continue. We wanted to develop a relationship with her, but we did not want her to see us as surrogate parents. We wanted her to develop into a great horse that could mix with other horses as well as with people. We wanted her to meet the potential of her breeding. We wanted her to be like her mother but yet be herself. In other words, we wanted to accomplish what doesn't usually happen with orphaned horses. Doesn't this sound like most parents when they talk about their children? The dreams are the same. Now it was up to us to sow the seeds and nurture her growth so Peanut could get the start she needed. We ended up setting the compass direction which would guide her through this early period and well through her life.

I will not say we did a good job with this horse, even though other people have said just those words, nor do we take credit for all she became. That was written before we began. We felt at times like we were around for the ride as she amazed us with her gifts. I will however, give a large amount of the credit to Owsley Farms for their breeding selection. Sam had a knack for choosing the right sire/dam combinations to get the best qualities in a foal and to ensure that the horse would coexist well with people. We had started several colts for Sam and found this to be true in every case. Peanut would prove to be even more exceptional. The balance of the credit, other than the small part we played, goes to this power surrounding us that we sometimes have difficulty sensing. I am thankful that throughout my later years, I have been gifted with glimpses of the possible and have become a true believer that all things can happen with hope, faith, and focus.

We built a reputation over the years of doing an extraordinary job starting colts. We took foals and started the process of socializing at an early age to ensure not only a bright future for the colts but also a safe future for their handlers. You need to keep in mind that most pleasure horses, as they mature, will end up weighing a little over one thousand pounds. The last thing you need to be around is a thousand-pound animal that has no respect or love for you. An untrained horse will not hesitate to use its hooves and teeth to their advantage in order to get away from you or to get you to leave them alone. Our job was to take nature's perfect prey animals, gifted with blazing speed and remarkable reflexes, and convince them to control their natural tendencies of fight or flight in order to be docile in the presence of humans.

This finishing process included teaching young colts to be respectful, lead, accept the halter, back up, be groomed, have their feet trimmed, load on a trailer, stall, tolerate being treated with fly control, give to pressure, and take shots. All these things and more are lessons that need to be mastered in order to get along with people. These are just the basics of coexistence between horses and humans. Many of these lessons would have been taught by the dam merely by being around her when she was around humans. Peanut could have learned simply by watching the interaction between us daily, but this possibility no longer existed. Or did it? Maybe it existed spiritually in a way that we could not sense with our limited abilities.

All of this training and finishing sounds easy in theory, but in reality it is usually anything but easy. Picture being handed a bag containing ten feral cats with instructions to turn the cats loose in an open field and then put them back in the bag—and do so within a prescribed time limit. Now you have an idea what it is like to start a lot of the colts we have trained. We measured success in small steps. For example, after haltering a colt for the first time, which can be a difficult feat, we start teaching them to lead. We pull on the lead with steady pressure until we get the smallest amount of forward movement from the horse. Then we stop the lesson having accomplished that really small first step!

With Peanut, small steps went by the wayside. She haltered and led like she had been doing it all her life. She never fought the lack of freedom. She apparently trusted me with all of herself, every time. She was not the first colt I trained, so I had many to compare her with. She was different than any of the others. You could see it in her soft eyes, which by now reminded me so much of her mother. She was trusting and relaxed. She was soft and compliant in her neck; never did she act tensed up or nervous. She felt loved and protected. She knew I would not ask anything of her that would hurt her.

I came to believe that something transpired the night that her mother died. Something spiritual, something older than time, some transfer of wisdom or spirit took place through the communication that we witnessed. Those readers who lean toward scientific rationale may disagree with me and call it by some other name, but I know what I believe.

The first time she had her feet trimmed, our farrier Ron Bryson could not believe this young horse. He said we did a great job getting her ready. We knew differently. She had become a total package not only from the start her mother gave her but also from the spirit which lived inside of her. That spirit was in the air the night her mother died. I believe that spirit raised her from the inside out. We might have directed the process, but she knew to trust us from the power within her. This was the gift from her mother, and that same power is available to all of us. We need to learn to let go and let it happen, whatever "it" is.

Peanut started her new life in the same barn lot or paddock where her mother died. She did not act like the place held any bad energy for her. She went through her training with flying colors and eventually learned to exist in a herd setting with ease. The sadness I felt at her beginning faded somewhat, and the hole left in my being by her mother's passing was filled with the love and respect I had for this little orphan filly. She and I developed the same exact bond that I had with Buffy, maybe even a stronger one. She would always greet me no matter the circumstances, seeming to say, "Hello, friend. How are you today? It is so good to see you. What might we talk about this time?"

And talk we did. I would stroke her head, neck, and shoulder much as I had done with her mother and talk the time away. I guess the words or stories didn't matter to her; it was the tone and cadence of my voice she found comforting. She was happy spending time around someone she shared a history with, even though it was a history that had its cloudy days. Ultimately, the good times far outweighed the bad, no matter how strongly the bad memories would try to dig in and set up residence. Reflect upon your life in this way. No matter how bad things seem to you, if you have faith in your soul's existence, the sun will shine and you will be able to smile with confidence.

The horse business can be happy or sad, depending on your outlook. We consciously try to choose the happy as often as possible, and when faced with the bad we choose not to give it the power of our focus. We are confident that we raised these young horses to have a good life and reach their potential. The foundation had been laid strong and sure. The process is not unlike raising a child, just shorter in duration. You know from the moment they are born that you will be letting go daily in small steps.

As we raised these horses for someone else, we knew they would eventually be sold. We also knew that when they left, a little part of us would always leave with them. The news finally came that Peanut had been sold to a breeding facility in Michigan named Miller Paint Horses, owned by Cheryl and Dale Miller. Peanut had been with us from the first breath she took. I was there the second she was born and would be there the day she was loaded on the trailer to leave.

Peanut was one of the very few young horses that had not been trained to load onto a trailer while she was here. Training funds had dried up, and I think subconsciously I hoped if I didn't train her to load, maybe she wouldn't go anywhere. So I was a tiny bit apprehensive the day she left. I think part of me was hoping she would throw a complete tantrum, refuse to get on the trailer, and choose instead to remain here forever. That was the parent in me, hoping for the Disney ending. But as always, life won out, and what was supposed to be, in the end, was exactly what happened.

True to her personality, Peanut loaded onto the trailer like she had been hauled every day of the two years she had been alive. It broke my heart, but she chose properly. She followed her spirit, ready to move on to a new experience. She once again trusted, holding nothing back. I have cried more than once over animals in my life, and suspect I have a few more heartbreaks to go, but I felt that the bond between us was and still is strong.

Peanut was an old spirit moving on to a new experience. She always seemed to know what to do and whom to trust, and she was always right. I moved on knowing I could visit Michigan and see her once again. After all, this is a small world we live in, made smaller everyday with advancing technology, and Michigan isn't that far away . . . right?

On September 20, 2011, I received a letter from Cheryl Miller. She wrote, "Just wanted to touch base with you to let you know Peanut is doing great!!!! We have started riding her and she has been perfect . . . never a buck or even a flinch!! She has the best personality and what a loving little girl. You did very well with her. " It was obvious that Peanut became what she needed to be, and she accepted that things are what things are. We all need to learn that.

Peanut's story doesn't end there, though. On September 30, 2011, I received an unexpected letter from Cheryl. She wrote, "Had to tell you, Ms. Peanut is also going to Italy!!!! They have been looking for well-bred mares and hoped to be able to breed them to our stallion before taking them to Italy. Well, they asked if we had any well-bred mares, and I told them about Peanut and also a Zippos Sensation mare we have in foal, and they took both of them. They are going to a beautiful horse farm, and even though I hated to part with them, they will have a wonderful life. Another saga in little Peanut's life!!!! I will keep you informed." The buyers were a couple who owned an equine facility in Italy. They were on a buying trip to American and had stopped at Miller Paint Horses to see another horse when they happened upon Peanut. The saga continues, and I am convinced once again that coincidence had nothing to do with it.

I found myself filled with mixed emotions. On one hand, the heartbreak I felt when Peanut left renewed itself and brought that sadness out of the file drawer in my mind where I hide such things, and it would be awhile before I could hide it again. On the other hand, what a wonderful adventure my little girl had in front of her. I wished her fair winds. I knew she would be fine. It is in her spirit to be strong and adventurous and to continue to follow her path.

The last communication I received from Italy via Cheryl was dated May 2, 2012. She sent the message to let me know that Peanut had entered yet another phase of her life. She was now a mother herself, of a very beautiful paint filly. She had adjusted well to her transition and as always was moving forward in her life. I know she carries her mother's spirit within her, and that spirit will be shared yet again with her daughter. And so the cycle of life continues as it has forever, as it will forever.

©2013 Horses seen through my eyes-by Agatha Kacprzak

My sister-in-law Elena is Italian. I contacted her for the correct translation for the title of this story. So I say *addio nocciolina*, good-bye Peanut. I will always keep you here in my mind. Our lives intertwining as they did made me a wiser person. The gifts I received from you and your mother are some of the most valuable I have ever received. The experiences we shared opened my eyes to the possibilities that surround me every day and brought a sense of peace to my being. For that, I thank you from the depths of my soul. Now I guess it is time to learn another language. I have to be able to communicate with Peanut's new keepers when I go visit her! Good-bye, old spirit. *Addio* to your aged soul that overflows with wisdom. Farewell young horse. Remember your lessons well. Keep your eyes soft and all knowing. I miss you. I always will.

Chapter Four

The Nature of Things

When mice run, cats give chase.
—Rachel Vincent

I T WAS A COOL, EARLY fall afternoon in Kentucky. My son, Matt, who was around seven at the time, and I were sitting on the patio enjoying a moment of rest after a hard day of work on the horse farm. I noticed Whiskers traversing the yard with something in his mouth. Like most barn cats that we have been the keepers of, Whiskers liked the house and yard much more than the barn. Being curious, I walked across the yard to see what he had captured and discovered that he had snared himself a chipmunk.

Now, I have to tell you I have a profound, lifelong love of chipmunks. I had captured one myself as a small child and kept it as a pet for a short time. He used to run up one arm and down the other like a blur. He would perch on my shoulder and eat peanuts from my hand. That was also the hand he bit one day, causing my parents to make him a wild chipmunk once again. It scarred my psyche, and I am not sure I ever got over it. I still loved watching them scamper about in search of seed and whatnot, but I lost all desire to make one of them a house pet again.

A couple of summers ago, I sat outside my in-laws' house in Maine for hours photographing the little seed-stealers as they came out from under the porch on their way to the bird feeders in their quest for an easy lunch. My in-laws love to feed their songbirds year round and have several feeders scattered about the yard. Blue jays, being the traffic cops of the bird world, would swoop down, land on the bird feeder, and scare the other birds away, albeit briefly. During this often occurring cycle, birdseed would fall to the ground in copious amounts. This is where the chipmunks and even some red squirrels entered into the fray. They would wait under the feeder and fill their cheeks completely, to the point of making their heads look hilariously distorted. They were so tame and used to people that I was able to take many pictures of their antics as they would fill their mouth pouches, leave for a little while, and then return empty once again to start anew. I never tired of watching their display.

Chipmunk, courtesy of Richard D. Rowland

I took the chipmunk, which I assumed was dead, away from Whiskers. The old barn cat was not real happy with my decision and followed me around the yard pleading mournfully in an attempt to have me reconsider my actions. The pleading led in short order to angry yowling, spitting, and downright demanding his way. You could tell from the glare he did not appreciate my siding with his prey. Whiskers finally relented and stalked off like a child, mad at not getting what he wanted.

Usually, I try not to interfere in such matters. Believe me when I tell you the ability to allow things to play out and not intervene too often is something I slowly developed later in life after facing my own challenges. I learned to appreciate the fact that nature has its means of checks and balances. I won't say I completely learned not to interfere, just that as my understanding developed, my rate of interference dropped considerably.

But I had seen how Whiskers would taunt his prey before dispatching it. Once I watched him torture a field mouse in the pasture behind the house. He would carry the mouse about thirty yards from the equipment shed and put it on the ground. Then he would walk beside it as the terrified creature tried his best to make it back to the safety of the shed, only to have Whiskers pick him up once again and start all over. After about four trips, Whiskers finally tired of the game and did as nature intended him to do. I will spare you the details, as I'm sure you already know the outcome.

After I took the chipmunk away from Whiskers, I held it in my hand for Matt to see what one looked like up close. As I opened my hand and Matt gazed at the apparently dead chipmunk, the unthinkable happened. The chipmunk took a huge gasping breath and seemed to magically return to life. I now realized the little fella wasn't dead after all but just playing that way in the hope his tormentor would put him down and forget him, something like what we are supposed to do to discourage a bear or mountain lion from eating us.

All of a sudden, I was holding in my callused hand a small, wild animal with very sharp teeth. Callused or not, those teeth could sink into my flesh easier than the wind flows through a leafless tree. Knowing this fact from first-hand experience, I hollered for Matt to get me something to put the chipmunk in. I knew if I put him down, Whiskers would once again claim him as abandoned property and the torment would start anew.

Matt quickly came back with a two-pound coffee can with a plastic lid. He had lined the bottom of the can with grass clippings and made a comfortable place for the chipmunk to rest and try to recover from his frightful experience. I deposited the little booger in the can and shut the lid before he could latch onto my fingers—or worse.

Before I had a chance to start the standard parental speech about wild things needing to stay in the wild, my son told me he wanted to keep the chipmunk as a pet and name him. He also reminded me he was having company for an overnight stay, and he couldn't wait to show them his chipmunk. I had to think quickly. I agreed that the chipmunk could stay long enough for Matt to gain bragging rights in front of his friends about how the capture occurred. After that, the little thing had to go back to his family, or they would miss him and wonder what happened to him. Matt saw the fairness of the situation and agreed with me. He had always been that way, a very caring and compassionate little man.

So I cut a hole in the plastic cover of the coffee can about one-quarter inch across so Chip (I told you Matt wanted to name him) could breathe, and we set him on the basement steps and went about our day. I never even considered that a chipmunk could get out of such a small hole. Looking back, I now wonder how many other times in my life my thought process did not travel forward quite as much as it should have in order to cover more of the possibilities that could arise from my actions.

As things turned out, I guess I should not have assumed Chip would wait patiently in his new yet temporary home while we showered and had supper. I know now it was something I should have considered. I envision the mentor I never had would have said something like, "Look for all the possibilities, young man, and prepare for them." Where the hell was my mentor when this happened?

Matt checked on our little friend just after dark to see if he might be hungry. He wasn't, as far as Matt could tell, because unfortunately there wasn't anything but grass clippings in the old coffee can home we had prepared for him.

You know, to us, our home is not very big. As a matter of fact, it is a rather small ranch-style house. But to a little bitty chipmunk, it was one huge hidey-hole with unlimited possibilities. I am sure he couldn't wait to get back to the rest of his family and let them know about their new house. His grandfather would be proud.

The worried search began. At the time we did not have a house cat, a lack that has since been corrected. So finding Chip was up to us. We started searching methodically throughout the house. We shut the basement door in the hope that we would trap him on one level or the other. We searched everywhere, one room at a time, shutting doors behind us and stuffing towels under the doors in order to block the cracks and deny access.

Can you imagine how many places there are in a house for a chipmunk to hide? I never gave it much thought either. Now I can assure you that there are far too many. We next took a broomstick and swept it back and forth under beds, behind the couch, behind the TV, and every other place we could not see behind or under in an attempt to scare it out of hiding.

Finally, the terrified little thing came out from behind the television, and the chase was on. I have never timed a chipmunk, but I am here to tell you, they are an actual blur when moving and can change direction much quicker than a fifty-year-old man can. However, my mindset was the same as it always had been: I would not quit until the deed was done. I kept chasing, and Matt kept directing and laughing. Yes, laughing!

Among the many things I have always loved about my son is his sense of humor, and I have never failed to keep him entertained. Thankfully, it was never the hurtful things I accidentally did to myself that he found humor in. You know, the knuckle-busting, glass-breaking, water-pipe-bursting things I did while being a master of the do-it-yourself. He never laughed at those mistakes. But he always laughed and I mean, "red in the face, couldn't breathe because he was laughing too hard" laughed at the profanity-laced tirades that followed those previously mentioned mistakes.

I have to admit here I am one of those people who used to have what my parents would call conniption fits when I did something wrong. Do you remember Darren McGavin as little Ralphie's father in *A Christmas Story*? He had nothing on me. I was the real master of the cuss word. I had a Doctorate Degree in Profanity. Had it been taught in college, I would have been an esteemed professor of the subject. I might have even had a building named after me. And my son appreciated my professionalism and my dedication to the art!

The conniption fit that followed was historic. I was tired of chasing that little booger around the house from room to room while not even coming close to catching him. Tired as I was, though, I was not going to give up. I was like a great white shark chasing after a speedily darting seal. This chipmunk was mine! I grabbed a dishtowel and renewed the chase, thinking I could throw the towel on top of him and even the playing field. Once covered, I thought I would have him where I wanted him. Quite the reverse was closer to the truth. The towel throws were in vain. I never came close to covering his furry little body.

I didn't mention that I had socks on, did I? We don't allow shoes in the house. This is a must when living on a horse farm. I don't even like to think about all I walk through during the course of a day, much less want to bring it into the house on dirty shoes. I was running at a pretty good clip, considering the size of the house when the Little Turd (affectionately calling him Chip was long past) cut hard to the left. I followed suit, but from there things did not go as planned. My feet sailed out from under me and my 195 pounds of solid muscle—well, maybe not solid, but firm—well not really firm, but this is my story isn't it? Where was I? Oh yeah, my 195 pounds of solid muscle hit the floor with a resounding *boom* that shook the very foundation of the house. I then slid across the kitchen floor and slammed into the wall. This caused the long, decorative, fake-cast-iron utensils which were mounted on the wall to come falling down, barely managing not to impale me.

At this point I was embarrassed and started into a red-faced, profanity-laced, completely out of control tirade that sent my son to his room with tears of laughter streaming down his face. He was laughing so hard he couldn't get a breath. I was worried—briefly. I really did feel terrible about the lack of control in front of such a young man—briefly. But I wanted that chipmunk out of the house immediately if not sooner. After all, on top of everything else, I had now been embarrassed and my tender ego bruised.

I called for Matt to prop the carport door open. I intended to herd the little booger right out the door. The chase resumed when I located the chipmunk hiding in the bathroom trying to catch his breath. It ran into the hallway, and I realized that the chase was almost over. He was headed for the open door. And out the door he went—right into the waiting jaws of Whiskers the barn cat, who apparently had been hiding under the truck and waiting patiently for this miscarriage of justice to be righted. Tail up, Whiskers rapidly headed off into the night with his prize.

With mouths agape, Matt and I stared at each other in complete disbelief. For just a moment in time, any possible humor in the strange ending of this situation was nowhere to be found. Then, the realization hit: things are what they are. What is supposed to happen will happen, one way or another. That night, Mother Nature prevailed. I did not give chase to Whiskers and gave up any thought of another rescue. We do not know the reasons for things happening as they do and may never know. I like to think someday we will, but as things stand now, it is a mystery. I have come to believe that there is no such thing as coincidence. All things are as they should be. Good, bad—makes no difference as long as the lesson is learned and we are able to grow spiritually and remember that we are immortal souls having a physical experience, not physical beings with a soul.

Now that a few years have passed, I can look back at this experience with a laugh. I have changed and no longer have the conniptions I used to have. Oh, I still have small ones, but I catch myself much quicker, thank goodness. I would like to think I have matured somewhat—although I'm not sure Matt and Jennifer would totally agree!

Chapter Five

The Circle Is Complete

*Life is as dear to a mute creature as it is to man. Just
as one wants happiness and fears pain, just as one
wants to live and not die, so do other creatures.*
—His Holiness the Dalai Lama

AFTER SARGE'S PASSING, I MUST admit to experiencing a fair
amount of guilt for his pain and death. I had many questions I was
asking of myself, questions which seemed to take up residence inside
my mind and beg for answers. This is how guilt seems to work for me,
it works its way inside my mind and becoming a constant, unwanted,
parasitic companion. Be careful of guilt, because it can take over your
thoughts and establish rule over you. I wanted to know if I did enough
during the early symptom phase of his life-ending illness. I wanted to
know why I assumed I would see him again the next morning after his
surgery. I wondered why we didn't have a proper good-bye. I wanted to
know how he came to get the disease. Was it food related? Since golden
retrievers seem to be very susceptible to bone cancer, is it something
man has brought about with our breeding practices? All of these and
many more guilt-induced thoughts seemed to be constant companions
as I moved about each day.

Then one day, out of the blue, I experienced an epiphany that led
me to the conclusion that feeling continuing guilt about something that

has already occurred and lives in the past is akin to building prison walls around your very being. Inside this wall, negativity reigns and flourishes. Pessimism and useless questioning swirl around constantly as they grow and create more of the same. Left unchecked, guilt can consume you. You will fail to remember all of the wonderful parts of your relationships with an animal—or people, for that matter—if you allow guilt to darken the light of goodness that surely existed as you traveled a path together.

The epiphany was this: the walls built by guilt have a locked door, but we possess the keys needed to unlock the door and escape the constant questioning we put ourselves through. The keys are forgiveness and acceptance. Use them and escape the guilt as I did. Forgive yourself the perceived wrongs planted in your mind by the guilt you experience and accept the notion that things are just as they should be. Focus on remembering all the good times and happy experiences you shared together. Stop the constant questioning of things you can no longer control. Learn from every experience and turn them into positives in your life. I escaped, and I moved forward armed with a new knowledge and a new mindset.

The circle that was broken when we lost our dog Sarge is repaired and working once again since the adoption of a dog from the local animal control center in Elizabethtown. Even though I made several trips to the shelter looking at dogs, in the end the choice was fairly easy. I guess you must take into consideration that this soft heart of mine wanted to bring all of the animals in residence at the shelter home, but my head won out. I only chose one.

I would estimate I made ten trips to the shelter over a five—to six-week period. I saw dogs of all breeds, including some questionable ones where you didn't have a clue what they might have descended from. I saw soulful-eyed beagles and a golden retriever that reminded me too much of Sarge. I saw shepherds of all kinds, hound dogs, a couple of pugs, too many mixed-breed dogs to list, and even a Chihuahua. Almost to a dog, they clamored for attention. They climbed the chain-link gates, barked, whimpered, and begged for consideration. Each one individually broke my heart, because I knew I had to pick one and one only.

During one visit, I stopped at a kennel with two dogs in it. Their breeding appeared to be the same and was described as a corgi mix. One of the dogs acted like all the others, wanting my interest so badly that it hurt me to only be able to give it a little attention before moving on to the next. But then I looked at the little black dog in the kennel with her. She didn't beg for attention, nor did she climb the gate trying to be petted. Part of me thought she appeared to be resigned to her fate, as this was not a no-kill shelter. Another part of me was wondering just what was going through this little dog's mind that set her apart from the rest. I surmised she was just a little above the begging stage, and resigned to death or not, she would not stoop to pleading with someone in order to gain a forever home. It is impossible to convince me that animals don't possess a very intuitive mind and know when they have been abandoned. I have witnessed the look on their faces when they have been abandoned, many times.

I inquired about her background and found out she had been at the shelter for five months, much longer than dogs usually make it before being disposed of or "put to sleep," as we try to state so humanely. Because she was such a sweet little dog, the employees knew that someday someone would take this dog home with them, and they couldn't bear to euthanize her. I had them get her out of the kennel, and she readily came to me and accepted petting. I then asked them to take her to the feline section so I could see how she acted toward cats. We have two barn cats and a house cat, and I just couldn't accept a dog that couldn't get along with cats. She did not pay any attention to the cats at all, just the people. After the brief visit was over, they put her back in her assigned kennel with the cold concrete floor, and she immediately returned to her distantness, viewing all that went on around her with a studying eye.

I made several trips back to the shelter but couldn't seem to get my mind off this little black mixed-breed dog. When I visited, she gave me all her attention, not to ask for rescue but as if to say, "Well are you ready to give this a try?" Finally, my decision was made. I filled out the adoption papers, paid the appropriate fees, and loaded the little girl in the truck. We were off to start the rest of her life and possibly mine too. Our eyes were wide open and our minds full of questions without apparent answers.

I wondered what circumstances brought her to the low point of her life of being in a kill shelter. Was she abused, neglected, or abandoned? Or, just maybe, all of those situational descriptions fit her circumstances. Was she lost? Maybe she ran from a car of interstate travelers as they stopped for a break from driving or as they made a pit stop for gas. She could have run away from home after being scared by fireworks or a thunderstorm, as some dogs are apt to do. My investigative mind leaned strongly toward the neglected or abandoned possibilities, since most people will try to find lost or missing pets they care about, and no one had inquired at the shelter about this little dog.

Why are some people so lacking in humanity, compassion, and empathy that they can take animals into their homes only to later abandon them without pause when it suits their needs? How can a person possibly open the yard gate and let an animal go, or drive one to the country and put them out of the car without benefit of food, water, shelter, love, or guidance? There are always other options! People need to arrive at the point where they realize animals have souls and feelings too. Hopefully, it is karmic, and abusers of animals will return to be abandoned or abused themselves. Let me close the door on this particular room of thought with this: When we humans domesticated wild animals such as dogs, cats and horses, we became the stewards of those animals. We are responsible for their welfare. Before abandoning those now unwanted animals, give them to a new family, or take them to a no kill shelter. Do something positive instead of shirking your responsibility. Try to etch this quote by Mahatma Gandhi in your mind for future reflection: "The greatness of a nation and its moral progress can be judged by the way its animals are treated." Do the right thing and not something that will later fill your heart with guilt. Trust me, as you age and face your coming mortality, your heart will soften, and you will reflect upon your life and the decisions you made. I hope you are able to like what you see.

It was Matt's turn in the rotation to name the next animal, a rotation that comes around much too often with people who have large hearts where animals are concerned. Cookie was the only word the little she-dog would respond to when she first came here, so it was a logical choice to name her that, and the name fit. Trust me, we tried all the common dog names to check for a response but only received a quizzical look for each utterance. So her moniker became what it is. What we normally called dog cookies now became dog treats. We just couldn't ask Cookie if she wanted a cookie, now could we!

We assume Cookie is a black corgi mixed with border collie maybe, but she might also be border collie mixed with one of the many herding breeds. She certainly has the traits of a herding dog. She was about two years old when we adopted her and has the body and ears of a corgi but with longer legs. Her feet and chest are tipped with white. She is not a replacement for Sarge, which would be impossible. She is a new chapter in our lives, just as we are a new chapter in hers. We do know that our paths crossed for a reason because she fits here. There are times when I think the little ankle nipper has been here always, and maybe in my mind she has.

Cookie has taught us something about adopted dogs—they can be fiercely loyal and protective. It seems as if they feel a debt to their new family for saving their lives and providing them with a loving home. I know, without hesitation, animals possess an uncanny ability to understand much more than we ever give them credit for knowing. Animals can be trained to the point of amazement, but beyond that they also can know, sense, and understand much more deeply than you think.

We run a small, family-oriented horse stable and have people in and out of the farm on a daily basis. Boarders arrive to ride and train their horses, delivery people travel the driveways, potential customers arrive for a tour of the facility, and some people volunteer their time here just to be around horses. Cookie goes to the barn with us and interacts well with all the above mentioned people. She is a little guarded but will let people love, pet, and scratch on her until they tire of it. She doesn't beg for attention but will accept what is offered, leaving as soon as the offer expires. This is life at the barn with this short little dog.

Her demeanor at the house is the polar opposite of her barn persona. The people who were welcome to ply Cookie with attention at the barn will be watched with a steely eye when they cross through the gate and enter the yard. When they observe this serious-minded little puffed up canine, people generally holler from the deck steps in order to get noticed rather than attempt knocking on the door. Some even call us on their cell phones before visiting. We listen closely for the arrival of guests in order to head off any problems and have so far maintained peace.

When you live in the country and have a dog, one of its jobs is to protect the family. You wouldn't want to yell at your dog every time they growl a warning unless you want to teach them everyone has good intentions, which we all know isn't always the case. The key in this matter, as with all things, is balance, and we feel we have arrived in the vicinity of the much-needed steadiness of that balance.

Otherwise, Cookie is a real sweetheart and seems to appreciate her new home. She is a bit shy at times, especially with men, or should I say me. Matt is six-foot-two and weighs in at around 235, and she is quite fond of him. She is also fond of Jennifer and, yes, the cat woman has found a soft spot in her heart for this little dog.

Cookie accompanies Jennifer to the barn each morning to feed the horses. The first few mornings were humorous for the barn cats. They didn't know what to think of the new addition. They frizzed up, arched, and spit, but Cookie paid them absolutely no mind as she went about the search and discovery of her new surroundings. That little show was an answer to prayers. I wanted a dog that left the cats alone, and this one fit the bill completely.

After a few days, Bill and Grace grew accustomed to Cookie, and now they all get along. We even have a picture of the three of them sleeping in the doghouse together. Yep, wishes granted, wants fulfilled. Digger the house cat took a little longer to adjust, but he came around after a spell and at times will play with Cookie in the yard.

Cookie gets along with other domesticated animals too, as well as some wild ones. A couple of the boarders will bring their dogs to the stables when they come to visit their horses. Cookie will run and play with the other dogs with complete abandon as if still a puppy at heart. She will also run interference for the birds as they eat at the feeders and bathe in the birdbath. If she sees one of the cats stalking birds, she will quickly run between the birds and the cat. The birds, seeing a dog charging at them, will leave for safer ground. As soon as this is accomplished, Cookie will return to what she was doing. I have seen this played out many times with the songbirds but never with other farm pests that the cats capture. I guess, for some unknown reason, she has a soft spot for our feathered friends.

Cookie also seemed to have a special connection with one dog that was here briefly. Not too long ago, on a Friday afternoon, I saw a dog on the side of the road next to the neighbor farmer's mailbox. I only caught a glimpse of it before it went into the cornfield. I didn't give it much thought, because this particular farmer had two Labs that sometime spent time around the road. Then I saw the dog again on Sunday and thought it odd, because I got a better look at it, and it did not look like a Lab.

On Monday, I called the farmer to inquire if it was his dog. He told me it wasn't and that he had called the animal control office to have it picked up. At this point, my soft heart started hurting for the injustices that occur around us at times and the need to make things right took over my being. It was strictly intuitive that I felt a strong need to intervene.

Monday night, Jennifer and I took some food and water to the area where the dog had been staying. The dog was not there at the time, so we left everything and called it a night. I thought here was a dog some uncaring person had dropped off on the side of the road for someone else to attend to. The dog was so loyal that he had waited right where he was dropped off, without food or water, for almost five days that I knew of, for that person to come back for him. This was an animal whose being was filled with devotion, and he deserved more of a chance in life than he had been given. I couldn't stand by and let him go to a kill shelter on the roll of the dice someone would adopt him.

Bright and early Tuesday morning, I returned and found the dog hiding at the edge of the cornfield. He had been there so long that he had a well-worn path off the side of the road to his lair in the corn and a bed wallowed out among the stalks. He was scared and shaking as I approached, but he didn't run. It took a long time to coax him out of the corn. I didn't have treats; all I had to offer was a soft voice and a mental promise to help him. I finally was able to slip a rope around his neck, and as I led him to the truck, he walked quietly beside me without pulling to try and get away.

I brought the dog, which had responded to the name Buddy, to the barn at our farm. The rest of the family plus Cookie met me there with food, fresh water, and a treat or two. Cookie let everyone love on Buddy and didn't seem to mind at all. She never once got in the way and had a funny look on her face the whole time. It was a caring and compassionate look that seemed to indicate she felt sorry for the dog. Cookie didn't want his fare. She didn't even beg for any treats to eat; she just sat and watched.

We had to put Buddy in a stall after he went after one of the barn cats. Whether he went after it playfully or aggressively I do not know, but I couldn't take the chance that it might happen again. Cookie would sit at the house and look forlornly at the barn. Occasionally she would walk over and sit with her body resting on the side of the barn, just outside the stall Buddy was in, as if to give him some company. It seemed she knew his plight and maybe at some time in the past had shared similar circumstances.

As much as we would have loved to keep this huge dog with the head of a golden retriever and a loving, loyal heart, we knew we couldn't take on another animal. We took him to the same no-kill shelter where we had adopted our barn cats. We made a donation large enough to cover his neutering, medical check, vaccinations, license, and worming, with enough left over to fatten him up. The big guy was adopted by a family with two daughters and a large fenced yard. Not that the yard size mattered, because they made him a housedog. Yep, Buddy got lucky, and little Cookie taught me her heart was full of concern and empathy for yet another species of animal.

Buddy, the abandoned dog

I think it is a plus to adopt animals from a rescue or shelter. You provide a home for an animal that otherwise might be put to sleep. Cookie had all her shots and was fixed, so the normal initial cost of pet stewardship was already paid in full. I told you earlier Cookie was a little distant, as if wanting you to make the first move toward a possible relationship. But after a brief transition, she lost that aloofness and has become part of this family. Who knows what this dog had gone through prior to finding a home with us? I have learned, as with all species including us, trust is earned, not given, and she mastered trusting us relatively quickly. She loves to be petted, scratched behind the ears and on her belly, and to be fed treats for learning. She also has an affinity for sleeping on her back in the yard, soaking up the warming rays of the sun during the day. It seems she has grown quite comfortable in her new home.

The rabbits have discovered the new addition and are thinning out a bit. In time, things will get to a new normal. Things usually do. The hole in my heart that Sarge's death left will grow smaller. It started to do just that one week after Cookie arrived here. When she didn't know I was watching, I saw Cookie roll in the grass, actually appearing to smell it, and heard her let out an audible sigh of contentment.

Cookie enjoying the feel of grass instead of a kennel

After five months in a kennel with concrete floors, the little things like a yard with grass to lie in, a loving word, a scratch behind the ears, and a job become big things in your life. I am glad we could provide a second chance for this little dog. I know she appreciates the opportunity and that Sarge is smiling down on her and us. I believe!

Chapter Six

An Unexpected Smile

In time of sickness the soul collects itself anew.
—Latin proverb

Used with permission Copyright 2012 Richard Small Photography

W HEN WRITING A BOOK SUCH as this one, the subject matter generally follows topics or related themes. At least half of this book revolves around the animal kingdom and how I believe we are interconnected. The other half describes the path I was on that gave life to these beliefs and made me aware of the diverse and interrelated life we lead. The following story may seem a little off topic at first, but the spirituality of the moment was strong. Ever since the day I had this experience, the story has begged to be told. It was one of those things that tugged at my sleeve while whispering in my ear, "This is important. Relay the message."

I did warn you previously I would not just write about horses, farms, and animals when I started this endeavor. I hope this writing will move you, maybe inspire you, and quite possibly cause some self-reflection. I know the experience that I am about to relay to you still makes me look upon things in a different way. So, please bear with the teller of the story and enjoy the journey.

This story took place in April, on a day when I had an appointment at the Veterans Hospital in Louisville, Kentucky. My healthcare had been entrusted to this institution for the previous five years, or since my latest journey had begun. The beginning of that particular day was extremely frustrating, and I allowed myself to be drawn into each offending drama by giving it the energy it needed to grow instead of remembering the phrase, "Things are what they are." I have gotten better at going with the ebb and flow of life and looking at living from a more peaceful place. But I started the day focused on my ego and me, and not the larger picture that we are all part of. This allowed the day to snowball into something that was almost unmanageable.

I always left early for these appointments because it is extremely difficult to find a parking space when valet parking is closed. I arrived an hour and a half before my scheduled time and got in the long, slow line for valet parking, a service that had been started because of a lack of space for handicapped parking and some other issues. Everyone is eligible to have their vehicles parked, and sometimes things run very smoothly, but it was not to be one of those days.

After a long wait, I was next in line for parking when they closed the service because no other spaces were available. The frustration that had started while I was waiting in line boiled over at that point as I took the perceived affront personally. Even though I could have stayed in line and waited for the valet parking to reopen, I chose instead to circle the vast parking area and try to find a space to park. I circled, circled, and circled some more. For an hour and ten minutes, I circled without finding a space to park, and all the while I was witnessing the valet line once again growing longer by the minute. With each circle of the parking lot, I was also growing angrier and more upset. Eventually, I gave up the search and returned to the valet line, to a position much further back than when I left it. My frustration grew, and it was totally self-imposed. I have always been one of those people for whom being on time means being five to ten minutes early, and I certainly wasn't going to make it inside at the hour I wanted to.

To add to my frustration, I tried to call the clinic where I had the appointment to let them know that I would be late, even though I was still relatively early. I called the clinic four times without getting an answer. Now I was not only frustrated but was feeling completely put out with the whole process and had started playing the "why me" card. I cursed the system, the bureaucracy of government healthcare, the terrible parking conditions, and my bad luck. I went as far as calling the office of the director of the hospital; after all, he had a poster in the entry of the hospital saying to call him if you have any problem. I certainly felt I had a problem. I got through to his office and was assured that the information about me being late would be relayed to the clinic even if they had to walk to the office and deliver the message in person. They also apologized for the difficulty I was experiencing. I think I got a little smug at this point. No, I am sure I was feeling smug.

Shortly after I ended my phone call, the valet parking reopened, and I finally moved forward, still frustrated and feeling completely put out personally without a thought for the dozens of other people who surrounded me and also had appointments. I never gave a thought to how many of them needed to get inside and be attended to because they were in much worse condition than I was. Nope, I only thought about me. After the day closed, I could look back and see just how self-centered and selfish my thoughts were, but at the time I saw nothing but my needs. Needless to say, as I look back, I did not like the "me" I was on that particular day. Can you relate? Have you had days or moments like I experienced where you failed to see the larger set of circumstances and only viewed how things were affecting you? If you are human, I bet you have, even if you do not want to admit it.

I checked in for my monthly visit and went to the waiting room to bide even more of my precious time waiting my turn to be poked and prodded. There were about six or seven people in the room with me. One was in a wheelchair. Looking back, I sometimes wonder if he was there at all. Maybe he was a visual message given life temporarily by the Creator to bring some calmness and a return to saneness to my life.

The previous year, I had a major back surgery and lost a lot of weight, to the tune of almost thirty pounds. During this recovery period in my life, I often described myself to others as a skeleton with skin stretched taught over its frame. After seeing the man in the wheelchair, I realized I never looked the way I had described myself because this man looked exactly like that, and fortunately I never looked as physically challenged as he did. He was sitting with his head in his hand, rubbing his forehead. He might have nudged the scales to seventy or eighty pounds at the most. It was impossible to guess his age—he might have been thirty or he may have been ninety. He had a small tuft of red hair at his crown but otherwise had little hair anywhere else. His left ear was gone except for the lobe. It was obvious this man was quite ill and didn't feel good that particular day. The gentleman was apparently by himself as there wasn't anyone sitting close to him.

If you ever visit any veterans' hospital, be prepared to see things that will affect you, will cause an emotional response whether you want them to or not, and sometimes, just maybe, will cause you to turn your head. It can be a depressing place. You will see people missing limbs, people with a variety of cancers from exposure to harmful chemicals, people with horrible burn scars, people with visible facial wounds of war, and people whose scars reside within their souls but show in the far-away look in their eyes.

Even though I have witnessed the horrors of war personally by being in a conflict, I am still surprised at the damage we humans can inflict upon others of our own species, not to mention the harm we cause to other beings in this world. All in the name of what—peace, freedom, ideological differences, support of allies? I have grown to believe the only excuse for war is the *last* excuse after *all* other avenues have been attempted and innocents are dying without relief or hope. As discouraging and shocking as a VA hospital can seem during a visit, it can also be a place of hope, a place of peace, and a place where people who have a shared past can feel understood and comfortable in their surroundings.

My eyes were drawn to this man in the wheelchair. Several times I remember hoping he would not feel my eyes upon him, and think I was morbidly staring. I wondered about his illness, his prognosis (even though I do not believe in doctor's crystal-ball guesses), and his very existence. I hate to repeat myself, but this man was obviously a very sick man. As I glanced at him, I wondered what was going through his mind as he sat and rubbed his forehead. Was he worried about his possible coming transition? Was he afraid? Was his physical and emotional pain too much to bear? What would my answers to those questions be if our roles were suddenly reversed?

Then, it happened. Whether he felt my eyes on him or just wanted to move from his position, he looked up and at me. He not only looked at me, he looked at me with the brightest blue eyes I have ever seen. His eyes were the only thing about him that did not silently scream woes, worries, and possibilities of a coming death. He looked me in the eye and unexpectedly smiled a most beautiful, peaceful smile and nodded his head. I returned his greeting with a nod and a big surprised smile.

After gazing at me for just a moment longer, he returned his head to his hand and started to rub his head once more. This man's nodded greeting and smile amazed me! With all of his many challenges, the fact that he could still smile at another human being and find joy in the return of a smile and greeting absolutely astounded me. That he could put his pain and worries aside for the briefest moment gave me hope for my future as well as the future of all of humanity. If only we all could learn that our bad days, our frustrations, our illnesses, our anger, and many other negatives only have power if we consciously decide to give them power.

We choose the emotions we allow to rule us. As easy and natural as it seems to give in to negative energy and to allow ourselves to become angry and frustrated when things do not go the way we want them to, we could just as easily reverse our reaction to doom with thoughts soaring with positive energy. You and I have the power to choose our reaction to life and the trials accompanying it; nothing else has that power. Use it well and wisely and see life's possibilities blossom before you.

The man's presence that day was an enlightening gift I will not soon forget. It made me more aware of the Creator and his wisdom. It made me realize that the line "Things are as they are" is so much more than just a line or a New Age thought. Things being as they are means acceptance and moving forward, not getting stuck wallowing in a pit of despair. It means we need to keep on traveling with the newfound knowledge and belief that we are eternal souls having a physical experience, not a body with a soul. We need to remember, "Breathe in, breathe out, move on."

His gift to me was to make me reflect upon my morning and my frustrations at the start of the day and to realize how minor my problems were when I compared my life to his. With his smile, this man taught me that if you take the time to look, you can always find others who are facing challenges greater than yours and doing just fine, thank you very much. It is all in how you perceive the mountain ahead of you. Do you see it as an insurmountable object that you dread having to expend the energy to climb over, or could you possibly see it as a beautiful creation filled with the history of eons that you can't wait to experience and see what is on the other side?

Shortly afterward, I was called in for my appointment. I left the waiting room wanting one more smile, but it was not to be. Later, I actually wondered if the man in the wheelchair was real or a message from the Creator to me—a message to accept frustrations, challenges, and change as part of this life we lead. Maybe it was a message to smile more often, whether you feel like it or not. Make eye contact with people and project a caring attitude. Be a beacon of hope for all you meet. The experience changed me and moved me, and I hope reading about it moves you. A simple, unexpected smile became a gift of awareness.

I am so very grateful for this thin man with one ear, bright-blue eyes, and a beautiful smile. He spoke to my heart without a word. He gave me strength and hope for all of us. Thank you, whoever you are, and peace be with you. Someday, we will meet once more and discuss that day.

Chapter Seven

Wild-Eyed and Laid Up

Permanence, perseverance and persistence in spite of all obstacles, discouragement and impossibilities: It is this, that in all things, distinguishes the strong soul from the weak.
—Thomas Carlyle

T HE FOLLOWING IS A FEEL-GOOD story told from the heart and as true as true can be. It is funny how certain dates will stick with me. This was one of those most memorable dates. It was on September 26, 2007, that I first met a horse named Pal who would change my life and test my belief in the possible.

As I've mentioned before, my wife Jennifer and I, along with son Matt, own a horse boarding/training/foaling farm in Kentucky, forty-some-odd miles from Louisville. We had been talking to a lady about boarding two horses for her, and the twenty-sixth was the day they would arrive at the stables. We knew ahead of time that they were special-needs horses, but we didn't fully realize the depth of their need or the challenges we would face in our attempt to return them to good health. Good health is just one of the goals we strive to reach. A great quality of life is the ultimate goal, but you can't have it without first mastering a return to good physical health.

The horses arrived early in the afternoon. It was a beautiful, sunny, early fall day as we left the house and started walking towards the barn to meet our new guests. The first one off the trailer was Sara. She was a twenty-seven-year-old American Saddlebred mare. She had a pretty sorrel coat, but pretty stopped there as far as a pleasing outward appearance was concerned. She was on the smallish side, standing 14-1 in height. For those of you unfamiliar with horse measurements, a hand is equal to four inches, or the average measure across your fingers when your palm is opened with fingers held together. So, a 14-1 high horse would be 57 inches tall at the withers, which is the peaked area on the back, right at the base of the neck. The bad news was that Sara's coat was extremely heavy and curly, which is a definite sign of Cushing's disease. You may have thought it was only a human problem, but horses can get it too. Sara led off from the horse trailer with her head held high, showing the regality of a much younger horse.

Next off the trailer was the horse that would test my abilities like no other. Pal was his name. He was at the time a fifteen-year-old Paso Fino. He had a beautiful golden palomino coat with a light-blonde mane and tail. He was also badly foundered. He was about as lame as I have seen a horse that was still walking, and his eyes were bright red where they shouldn't have been. He had an eye cancer on his left eye about the size of a marble that made him look wild-eyed. I am telling you, he looked almost demonic. In front of the barn, where no others horses could see him, he limped slowly off the trailer, following behind his friend Sara.

Pal showed his extreme discomfort until we put him in the riding arena. We generally put horses there when they first arrive at the stables. Being centrally located, this gives them a chance to nose over with the other horses at the stables and gives us an idea of where we are going to put them. Horse politics play into decisions regarding placement in fields. In this case, politics is another name for dominance in the herd. We study where horses appear to fall in the pecking order before placing them so we have less drama to work around.

After a limping Pal made it into the arena, his whole demeanor changed. His head came up, and he stepped out proudly. I must digress here a bit to tell you a little about males. We do not like to show weakness in front of other men. We could be bleeding to death, but we would still try to move about so as not to appear weak in front of another man, saying "I'm good" over and over. It is a man thing. It is also a horse thing. Weak horses will be culled out of the herd by the herd so as not to endanger it. We men save exhibitions of weakness up and display them in front of the women in our lives, whether it be it our mothers when we are young or our wives as we age. They bear the brunt of this banking of pain we men have mastered. Ask any woman who is sharing space with a man who has a cold or a splinter, and they will tell you what I am talking about.

Pal did not want to show any weakness in front of the other horses, so he stepped out proudly. Even though he was in extreme pain, he did not show it. He taught me a little lesson that day, and he would go on for years teaching me lessons. He showed me where his heart was, and he showed me he had the drive and the "want to," both of which would be needed to help us accomplish what we had to do order to save him. He had no give. This wild-eyed horse still wanted to shine in someone's eyes. I vowed that day to do everything I could to make sure this was exactly what would happen. The challenge was accepted, and we started moving forward.

On October 26, just a few short weeks after the new charges arrived, Sara unfortunately had to be put down. In addition to the Cushing's disease, she apparently had an undiagnosed bone cancer. Sometime during the night, her shoulder had broken. She spent the night cutting a trench in the earth with her hooves in an attempt to get up, but it was not to be. Dr. Chad Bailey arrived shortly after being called, along with the owner, and Sara's misery was ended. Twenty-seven years is a good run for a horse. Most will live thirty to thirty-five years, and I know of some horses that have lived into their forties.

Miss Sara's pain and suffering ended that day, but Pal lost his buddy and his life had to start anew. He went at it like everything else he did in life, with a great attitude and the need to shine. Unfortunately, he could not stop the founder he was experiencing. He had another bad flare-up that brought major changes his way.

≈

I guess it is time to tell you about founder. Basically, founder is the name given to severe cases of laminitis, which is a swelling of the soft tissue in the hoof between the hoof wall and the end of the leg bone. The swelling has nowhere to go, and the laminae in the hoof can die. Depending upon the degree of founder, a small bone at the end of the leg bone called the coffin bone can rotate and actually come out the bottom of the hoof. This is the extreme, but you get the idea.

Many things can cause founder: chemicals, excess feed, lush green grass, stress, and more. Once a horse has foundered, it is much more susceptible to reoccurring bouts with the disease. Proper nutrition is the key to keeping flare-ups from occurring. We have developed a proprietary blend of feed in order to address the nutritional needs of a foundered horse. They get nothing to eat but what we feed them. Neither a peppermint nor an apple slice will pass their lips.

This diet also addressed the issue Pal had with the eye cancer. Jennifer and I are believers that proper nutrition is the key to battling any disease, and most diseases are caused by poor diet. In this case, fortunately, we were right. Within two months of becoming what the industry calls a "dry lot horse," Pal was cantering, bucking, farting, and generally having a good time. The surgery that was scheduled to address the eye cancer was cancelled because the eye cancer was gone. That is right—gone! There was no sign of it ever being there. His eye color came back, his coat glistened, and he regained the beautiful appearance of his youth.

Just to explain, a dry lot horse is a horse that cannot be on pasture. The sugar content in our pasture grasses here in Kentucky is extremely high. Sugar is a definite no-no for the foundered horse. They spend their lives during three of the seasons in dry lot. Pal lives in a corral-like setting which has a chute that goes into a stall. It is only during the winter that he can go out in the barn lot. Basically, he is an inside-boarded horse.

This is generally a much more expensive situation for the owner. We love this horse so much that we lose money on him monthly. The owner does help a lot with the more expensive feed he is eating, but it does not offset the high cost of his feed, supplements, bedding, and the like. A full board is just a lot more expensive than a horse boarded in a pasture. I never said I was a good businessman. My heart is too big to try to make a profit from Pal's situation, so we only charged the owner the same amount as outside board plus a little toward the feed rations.

The owner has a big heart also. Pal belonged to her father. He was a one-man horse, and the two of them were quite the pair until he died, leaving Pal rudderless for a while. I have heard so many stories about Pal and his first keeper. I really don't think we own horses but instead share time with them and take care of them, so I generally refer to people as keepers, not owners. The stories I was told about Pal and his keeper's prior life gave me a lot of insight into Pal's personality.

Pal has a playful side to him. He is mischievous. He loves attention of any kind but especially enjoys playing tag. I get in the round pen and dart in different directions, and Pal will come after me and then dart away. He never tires of it. He gets a funny look in his eye when we play, like he is trying to fake me out, and he usually does. He also loves my goatee. I will put my chin on his muzzle, and he will move his muzzle up and down in order to slightly scratch it. This is not something I would normally recommend that people do, as horses can and do bite, and the bites can be severe. But I do a lot of things with Pal to make him feel like he has something to look forward to. Being a dry lot horse is a very limiting existence.

Pal is also a great conversationalist. I have often said some of the best conversations I have ever had were with a horse. There is something about the cadence and tone of your voice that keeps them right there beside you, seemingly enthralled with what you have to say. I have even had some put their head over my shoulder and listen as long as I would talk. Pal loves it when you talk to him. During some of our conversations, I would make promises to him. I made promises of a relatively pain-free life, promises of a return to some freedom, and promises of a high quality of life. Now I had to keep my promises.

It was during these games that I had my first experience with the previous keeper, the one I said had passed away prior to Pal coming here. On two different occasions, out of the corner of my eye, I saw someone watching me. It happened once while playing tag with Pal and once while grooming him. If you have never experienced such a thing, let me tell you it is hair-raising. The person was about my height and was wearing a light flannel shirt, blue jeans, and a baseball type cap. There is no doubt in my mind that I saw this person, but when I looked directly at the image, he faded away.

After talking to the owner's daughter, I was convinced that her father had paid me a visit to see how his horse was being treated. She described him as I saw him, even though I had given her no hint of what I had seen. I merely asked her to describe her dad. I told my wife about one of the experiences, and she told me she had also seen him. We firmly believe such things are possible.

As I said, Pal's owner has a big heart, but she is a single mother with a demanding job. Her time was limited, and we understood her situation. So we quite willingly made the decision to become Pal's complete caretakers. His owner pays the board and comes on farrier day, but we manage all other aspects of his life. We try to fill his life and make him feel like he shines in someone's eyes just like he wants to.

Pal looks forward to his grooming. Jennifer took that task on after I once said I was going to cut his mane because it was too long. She has seen what horses look like after I give them a haircut, and she didn't want Pal to look like that. I am sure he didn't want to either. See, we men have our ways to get out of things sometimes.

Pal shows off his fancy new "do" thanks to Jennifer

Matt takes care of Pal's stall. I have no doubt that he gets quite put out with Pal, because Pal refuses to do his business outside. He cannot wait for the stall to be clean so he can go to the bathroom. I sometimes think it is another of his games. I can actually envision a smirk on his face when he messes up a newly cleaned stall knowing the reaction he'll get from its cleaner. Kinda warms my heart and brings a smile to my face.

≈

I knew in my heart that all of the things that we had done for Pal had not been enough. We felt we were allowing ourselves to be limited by his condition. So, we worked and worked hard to make him even better. We had a goal in mind, and we hoped it was a goal that would make him grin. We wanted him to be in such good condition that he could be ridden again. This was definitely a far-reaching goal. A nineteen-year-old horse that was foundered as badly as Pal surely couldn't be ridden again, could he?

We had been through the early months of disappointing flare-ups, some so bad that the owner asked if it was time to put him down. We made an untold numbers of changes to his diet, including some that left him too thin. But we had now finally reached a point where it was time to try. The first thing we had to come up with was a low-sugar, slow-metabolizing supplement to put a little weight back on him. Pal had lost some muscle mass, so this took a while. But finally the day came to see if our endeavors were going to pay off.

On September 17, 2011, almost four years to the day since Pal had arrived in our lives, Jennifer put a saddle on him. At first, we were just going to judge how he acted. And he acted like he was saying, "Let's *go*!" I couldn't believe it. After all those years, he was ready. One of our boarders, Lee Graves, who has no fear, rode him first. Pal never acted up at all. It had been a total of about eight years since anyone had been on his back. He rode like he had just finished his training. He reacted to leg controls, voice commands, and the reins. Whoever trained him did a great job, and Pal had not forgotten a thing. Jennifer rode him next and loved the way he responded. Pal was a gentleman, and you could tell by his demeanor that he realized once again, he was shining in someone's eyes—in all of our eyes, in fact!

Jennifer on Pal for the first time

Since that day, Pal has been ridden several times, sometimes in the arena and sometimes in the round pen. He just keeps getting better and better. He loves having a job again. All of the animals domesticated by humans want a job to do. Well, maybe not all cats; we have three that are good mousers but only when the notion hits them. Pal was no different in his desire for something to do on a regular basis. He often stares at the house, waiting for someone to come get him and take him for a ride.

I believe that someday he will be able to go outside of the arena and round pen to the real world. He will have to wear a muzzle to keep him from grazing, but once again he will taste freedom. We have come back around. I have kept my promises to him. With the help of the Creator, we have made him well enough to have a good quality of life, to be able to work and play without the extreme pain he was feeling. I myself am stronger from watching this horse move forward, always forward, after all the challenges he faced.

I went through a health scare the year after Pal came here to live. I was able to apply what I learned from him to go forward myself, and I believe I learned it well. The analytical part of me used to relentlessly search for answers scientifically as to why things happen. I always had to have an answer to the question why. I am glad this drive has dimmed and I can now accept that sometimes things cannot be explained by science. I have had many spiritual experiences science cannot explain, but the inability to understand my experiences scientifically certainly does not make them any less real to me.

In the late fall of 2011, Jennifer and I had a conversation about Pal. It seemed we both had once again unknowingly been having the same thoughts. It is a little funny how closely we are connected. There are times I will be thinking about something, and then she will mention it without my speaking out loud about the subject, and the reverse also occurs with regularity. In addition, there are other times when we finish each other's sentences, have the same desires for dinner, or out of the blue speak about the same subject at the very same moment. I know other married couples experience this phenomenon as well, because I have heard them mention it. This connection we have is strong!

The conversation we had about Pal concerned the possibility of us adopting him and accepting sole responsibility for his welfare. The conversation came out of the blue. We decided that if we were solely his keepers, we would feel a little more comfortable pushing the limits of his comeback and allowing him more freedom. We also gave thought of the fact that we lose money on him every month, and if we were going to lose money on him, we would rather he just be our horse, thereby, taking business out of the equation.

Later that week I had a conversation with his owner and told her we were willing to adopt him and give him a forever home if she were willing to let it happen. We promised to take care of him as her father did and to see to all of his needs. So, on November 29, 2011, Palido de Faeton, Pal's registered name, born May 25, 1992, officially became part of our horse family and will remain here as long as he lives.

On December 10, 2011, Pal's personality joined forces with the social media network of Facebook. Pal has his own site called Pal's Page. We introduced him as the owner of the page, and he communicates with people who make comments and leave messages for him. It is his personality that comes out on the page, which I describe as a little goofy and sometimes gooberish. Yes, I know that isn't a word, but it fits him completely. Where my personality comes across as more spiritual, deep, and calm, his is quite the opposite, always looking for the humor in things, being flirtatious and silly. As of this writing, he has around 1900 fans, some of whom interact with him daily. It has become another medium for us in our efforts to communicate to others the message that founder is not the end of a horse, cancer can sometimes be treated with nutrition, and you need to move forward through each day while facing your challenges with humor and hope.

Learn this lesson: things are what things are, all is what it is supposed to be, and all is well. I have learned these things, and I have been at peace ever since I learned to live in this very moment in time. Right now is all there is. Embrace it and enjoy it.

Chapter Eight

The Effects of Choice

When you make a choice, you change the future.
—Deepak Chopra

A Chance Meeting

STORIES SPEND A LOT OF time bouncing around inside my mind before ever making it to the point of being written. Even though this is not the last story chronologically in Part One of *Unspoken Messages,* it is the last story I needed to write in order to complete this book. All of the other stories had already been written, rewritten several times, and polished before being sent to the editor. The process itself was lengthy and time consuming but well spent and I guess you could say somewhat cathartic. I suppose the reasons for waiting until the end to write this accounting might have been related to the amount of research I needed to do before starting the project. I also felt my writing style needed to mature and level out somewhat. I hope this story will entertain you and that you will experience some "aha" moments as you read it.

I would like to start by defining two words that can be used to explain things that can occur in your life which may on the surface seem a little odd. Are these odd events that occur strictly coincidence or are they part of something else, some larger plan that surrounds each of us in the universe? The words I am talking about are *serendipitous* and *synchronicity*.

According to the online version of *The American Heritage Dictionary of the English Language,* the word *serendipitous* is defined as:

1. The faculty of making fortunate discoveries by accident.
2. The fact or occurrence of such discoveries.
3. An instance of making such a discovery.

The word *synchronicity* is defined as:

1. The state or fact of being synchronous or simultaneous; synchronism.
2. Coincidence of events that appear meaningfully related but do not seem to be causally connected, taken by Jungian psychoanalytic theory to be evidence of a connection between the mind and material objects.

I want to throw one more definition at you before we shut the dictionary, or in this case, "close the window." I feel it is important to define coincidence from the same source as, "A sequence of events that although accidental seems to have been planned or arranged." There you have the basis for this story. Are things merely coincidental in life, or do things happen just as they are supposed to happen?

It was in the early autumn of my life that I made a decision to start an equine-related business. I consider my autumnal years to have started at the age of fifty, a time when I was searching for something meaningful to do with the rest of my life. The decision came at the urging of a friend who had rekindled my lifelong love for animals of all species, especially horses. After purchasing the house and land where we still live today, I spent a couple of years building fences and buildings, renewing pastures, leasing more property, and establishing contacts. I intended to raise, train, and sell horses using my own methods.

It was through those contacts that I met a cowboy named Bob Littlefield. Calling Bob a cowboy is the highest compliment I can pay a man in this business. He was also a respected member of the horse community. I let Bob know I was in the market for some well-bred broodmares from which to raise future foals. I didn't just want outstanding breeding lines; I also wanted well-trained horses.

When you deal with horses on a daily basis, you gain a high respect for horses that interact with humans well, so that was high on my list of wants when it came to buying horses. It is also a trait I like to see passed on to the future generations of horses through the mare. When you see the term "broodmare," most people picture them as horses used strictly for the purpose of having babies and nothing more. What I envisioned in the horses I purchased were horses that, along with having babies, could also be used for lessons, trail riding, or even working with people to help them overcome a fear of horses. It was a tall order, but Bob headed me in the right direction.

Bob called me late in the afternoon on September 7, 2001, concerning what would be the second mare he wanted me to consider. The previous month, I had purchased my first mare through Bob. Annie was what we called her, and she was turning out to be all I had been looking for in a horse. Bob told me he had a pretty good mare he felt I should consider buying and she would be at his barn later that evening if I were interested. He recited her breeding while we were on the phone. I was impressed, so I agreed to meet him and the owner of the horse at his barn later that evening.

I arrived at the barn well after dark and was met by Bob, his wife Dee Dee, the current owner Trent Dorsey, and a dark sorrel-coated horse we would end up calling Pearl. The mare had the softest eye I had ever seen. A soft eye, in my mind, is a sign of calmness and a showing of confidence by a horse that knows its place in the world.

There is a method to buying or selling a horse. At the beginning, it may seem like you are just engaging in small talk, but in reality you are picking the mind of the other person regarding questions and concerns you may have and answers you seek. You also get a feel for the honesty of the other person, which weighs greatly in the decision making process. Knowing and trusting Bob as I did helped put Trent higher on the list of people I could have faith in, and nothing I discovered during our conversation made me think differently. He was extremely knowledgeable about horses, training methods, bloodlines, and especially that particular mare. He owned her dam. He was there when she was born, and he raised her, broke her to ride, and trained her. Now he was going to sell her.

The next step in the process was to slowly go over every inch of the mare looking for injuries, scars, hot joints that could indicate inflammation, ruptured tendons, and a great many other physically viewed issues could indicate future problems. Then you judge the horse's reaction to your movements and see how well she has been trained in ground manners, how she gives to pressure, and how respectful she is when in the presence of humans. These are just the highlights of a long list of checks. Suffice it to say, Pearl passed totally in all categories.

The final step in the pre-purchase process is to see the horse ridden. Rarely would I ever consider buying a horse that the owner would not ride in my presence. The only time I would suspend this rule would be if the current owner could not physically ride anymore due to health issues or if a deceased family member of the seller had previously owned the horse. I asked Trent if the mare rode well. He replied, "Well, she hasn't been ridden in over six months, but I think she'll do just fine." With that he grabbed some mane and mounted the mare. Pearl only had on a halter and a lead rope. In most cases when riding horses, you would have the horse tacked out with a bridle, bit, and reins in order to control them properly.

Trent had Pearl do some reining spins to the left and some reining spins to the right and then come to a halt facing me. A reining spin is a movement horses make by spinning in a tight circle while pivoting on their back feet. After that display, Trent had her back up about twenty feet, turn around 180 degrees, back up once again the same distance, and then turn to face us right where she started out. I was trying to hide the look of amazement on my face during this display of horsemanship and communication in order to keep him from knowing the sale was all but final, but the show was not over. He proceeded to have her side-pass to the left and back again to the right. In a side-pass, the horses walk sideways by crossing their legs and stepping under, keeping their body in a straight line and moving to the side. Trent and Pearl then did an abrupt turn to the left and rode off into the darkness. I was left behind with my mouth agape and my eyes wide open in surprise and admiration for what I had just witnessed.

Keep in mind that all of these moves were accomplished without the aid of reins or any other tack-related controls. They were preformed strictly with body language and leg pressure. No voice controls or verbal cues were used to indicate what was wanted of the horse. Trent and Pearl soon returned, and the dickering, the final step in this particular dance, began. In the end, I couldn't talk him down and shouldn't have even tried. She was worth every penny he was asking for her. On a handshake the deal was made; I had just purchased the horse that was to become my favorite riding horse and my best friend for several years to come.

Please know the decision to buy Pearl was based on the total package and not just the display of horsemanship. The softness of her eye and respectfulness when she was around me made the decision easy. The rest was like polish on my favorite saddle: it makes it more pleasing to the eye, but how well the saddle is constructed and how comfortable it is are the most important things. Trent agreed to deliver Pearl the next day and asked for directions to my farm. When I gave him the directions, Trent got a funny look on his face that I couldn't decipher and said, "I am pretty sure I know exactly where your farm is. I will see you tomorrow morning." And with those words, the night ended, and I returned home high on hopes and future plans.

A Homecoming

The next morning, I arose at an early hour, as is my habit. I couldn't get the look I had seen on Trent's face off my mind. Had I somehow, unknowingly been hoodwinked? I played the events of the previous evening over and over without coming to a solution that would quiet my mind.

Trent arrived around nine in the morning with a horse trailer in tow. I met him at the barn and noticed the look I had seen the night before had been replaced with one of pleasant surprise. It was the kind of look you get from someone who knows a secret you don't know, but they are about to share it with you.

Trent said, "When you gave me directions last night, I thought the location sounded familiar. I bought this mare's mother from a Mr. Heady at this very farm, and the mare I bought was in foal with the horse you just bought. The mother was called Double Bid and was the favorite riding horse of Mr. Heady."

The horse I had just purchased was conceived on this very farm some years ago and had returned home. I must reaffirm here that I do not believe in coincidence. This was something that was meant to happen for reasons yet unknown to me. The look on my face now mirrored that of Trent's, a look of total surprise. We made small talk as I introduced Pearl to her pasture mate and her new home. Shortly afterward Trent went on his way, but our paths would cross many more times over the years. I have a lot of respect for him as a person and for his horsemanship skills.

The Mr. Heady who Trent spoke of was my friend Bob Heady. Bob was my neighbor in our local farming community and had previously owned the farm where I reside. He also raised, trained, and sold horses as a sideline. From previous talks, I knew his favorite riding horse had been a horse he called Double Bid. Every time he would tell me stories about his horse, he would get a faraway look in his eyes, and occasionally they would mist over. I would come to know that feeling very well in my future. I couldn't wait to see Bob and relay the news about my new purchase.

Bob Heady would have been about eighty-six or eighty-seven years old around the time these occurrences were taking place. He was a small yet spry man who cast a huge shadow. He and his wife Edna lived on a parcel of land adjacent to our farm. We had become very close friends in the three years since I bought the place, and he was happy that once again there would be horses on the farm.

Bob had spent his life around horses, and oh the stories he could tell. He would mesmerize me with tales of long ago and his life with horses. These tales ran the gamut from the time he turned over a buggy while showing off for the girls as he arrived one morning for high school classes all the way to breaking his last horse at the ripe old age of seventy-two, in the breezeway of the barn where I now live. A barn's breezeway is the aisle that runs down the center of a barn, which you see when the back and front doors are open. Bob said this was the easiest place to break a horse to ride, because they didn't have anywhere to go and nothing to do but learn what you wanted. It was also the coolest place to sit in the summertime when the heat outside was unbearable. I learned so very much from this man because of his lifetime of experience.

I couldn't wait to let him know about Pearl, so it didn't take me long to call him and let him know I was coming by for a visit.

Although I had been an acquaintance of Bob Heady's for years, our friendship took off and grew stronger after I bought his old farm and continued what he had started. As we grew close, he became my mentor. He would even spend nights in the barn with Matt and I at foaling season during his late seventies and early eighties. I guess we became close enough that he could even be comfortable crying in front of me, but it only happened twice.

This was to be one of those times. I arrived at his house early in the morning with the registration papers in hand, ready to tell a story and hopefully touch a memory. I said, "Bob, I bought another horse this morning, and I thought you might be interested in seeing her bloodlines."

As I handed him the papers, he said, "Well let's take a look and see what you've found." He put his reading glasses on and started reading the information. I watched him and could detect a hint of disbelief and surprise in his eyes as he read. I could also tell when he stopped and started reading the registration from the beginning once again. When he finished, he looked at me with tears in his eyes and said questioningly, "She has come home?"

I answered that she had indeed and she was at the barn if he would like to visit with her.

As I was talking, happy tears ran down his cheeks unabated. He then started telling me stories about how Pearl's dam was his all-time favorite riding horse, which I already knew! Out of respect, I did not remind him I'd heard the story several times before. He went on to tell me how hard it was for him to make the decision to sell her due to his failing health. He thought she deserved to have an owner that could do with her what she loved to do, which was travel anywhere and everywhere. He told me the horse I bought was the last one he oversaw the stud selection and breeding of, and it always hurt him that she was not foaled here.

We then went to the barn, where for hours he oohed, aahed, and cooed to this horse that had come from the old Heady line. He then happily returned home to tell Edna the tale. Bob loved a good tale, and he loved repeating them. He also became a frequent visitor to see Pearl and was here when she had her babies during the years to come. I will live the rest of my life convinced that this mare returned here, using me as the means, to bring some peace to Bob's last years and to rekindle his memories of long ago.

I really believe that I could write a book about my relationship with Bob Heady and all I learned from him, but I will just tell about the one other time I unintentionally made him cry and leave the rest for perhaps another day. During the month of October in Bob's ninetieth year, Jennifer and I decided we wanted to give Bob another gift. Bob needed another heart surgery, which would have been his second major one, but he had opted instead to live the rest of his life as he was rather than go through another physically taxing recovery. He knew that, for him, this life's trail ride was reaching the end.

We wanted him to have one last horseback ride. Annie was and is still our most trusted horse and someday deserves her own story. We knew anyone could ride Annie safely, and neither of us had an ounce of fear that anything bad would happen. It would have been wonderful if Bob had been able to ride Pearl, but she was in foal and already showing pretty good. So we decided to let Bob have his last ride on Annie.

It was an absolutely beautiful fall day in Kentucky when we had Bob stop by under the premise of showing him something. I knew he would be attired in a way conducive to riding horses, because that is how he dressed every day, right down to the cowboy boots. He did not let me down either; he arrived dressed to ride horses and work cows. We told him what we had in mind, and he never once hesitated. His face took on a childlike expression of surprise and glee as he envisioned the fun ahead. We had Annie saddled up, and Jennifer helped Bob into the saddle. She then grabbed the lead rope and started to lead Bob and Annie around the round pen.

I will never forget what came next as Bob looked Jennifer right in the eye and said, "I think I can handle it from here." Handle it he did! He moved Annie into a walk, a trot, and a sustained canter. Now, Annie is a safe horse, but she is basically a lazy horse. That is what makes her so safe. She didn't get in a sustained canter for anyone, or I guess I should say she didn't until that day. She did exactly what Bob wanted and asked of her, and they both looked beautiful dancing together, an aging cowboy and a trusty Quarter horse. Bob put his horseman skills out there for all to see. Round and round they went for about twenty minutes, changing pace, stopping, backing, and going again. Bob put Annie through the paces until they both had had enough fun. Bob dismounted like a twenty-year-old cowboy instead of the ninety-year-old that he was, and his smile went from ear to ear.

We wished him a happy birthday and a good life as he headed home to tell Edna of the day's adventures. And do you know what? Edna did not believe him until we had the photographs developed and showed her pictures like this one. Her reply? "The old fool, I didn't think he would take chances like that anymore." Jennifer, Matt, and I all smile every time we remember this day and the memories it etched in our minds.

Bob's last ride on Annie

What made Bob cry for the second and last time in front of me was not the occurrences of that day but rather something I did concerning those occurrences. I wrote a short article about everything that occurred during what would come to be Bob's last ride and submitted it to the *American Quarter Horse Journal* along with a picture, and they published the story.

I bought several copies of the magazine to have on hand, and I took a couple to Bob's house one morning. The old cowboy that only three months previously had been dancing an energetic jig in the middle of our kitchen was now pretty much relegated to the bed or couch because of his failing health. He slipped on his familiar reading glasses and read the article a couple of times and gazed at the picture with tears running down his leathery cheeks.

His shoulders shook as he sobbed and thanked me profusely for doing what I had done. He said it was a highlight of the long life he had led. And I must admit, I cried with him, because I realized my larger than life friend would soon be transitioning to a place we all must go eventually. He was going home. He did promise me he would try to hold on long enough to attend the September wedding of Jennifer and me, but he did not make it. Bob died before his ninety-first birthday, leaving behind a wealth of friends, family, and memories that will carry on forever.

Our wedding was held as scheduled in September of 2005. The ceremony took place in front of the barn where we had met four years previously. The wedding had a Western theme, and we were on horseback. Jennifer rode Jackie and I rode Annie. (Pearl was down with a hoof infection and couldn't be ridden that day.) You would think an early fall wedding in Kentucky would be the ideal time to have an outdoor wedding. It turned out to be an extremely hot day without a hint of a breeze, which was very uncharacteristic for late September. I mean there wasn't any air movement at all, and everyone in attendance was sweating bullets.

About midway through the marriage ceremony, the doors at the barn adjacent to the one we were in front of opened wide. There was no breeze to blow them open, plus they had been latched. And when they opened, they opened with a loud creak on rusted hinges. Jennifer and I both looked knowingly at each other from the backs of our horses. Bob had kept his promise—he made it to the wedding. The spiritual place I was heading mentally toward and the place where Jennifer had already arrived made that belief possible.

A Name That Changed

When Pearl arrived in our lives, her registered name with the American Quarter Horse Association was Kate Bar Bid. Her normal moniker would have been Kate or Katie. However, as much as I loved the name, we already had a horse on the farm named Kate, and she belonged to Matt. We didn't feel it would be right to have two horses with the same name, so we needed to come up with something to call this horse. As I mentioned previously, we take turns naming the animals that we become stewards of, and it was Matt's turn to name this one. He and I have an affinity for old-fashioned names, and Kate Bar Bid's new name became Pearl for reasons unknown to me other than its antiquity.

It turned out to be a name that matched her totally. She was a rare horse to be around because of her immense intelligence and physical abilities, and she had a personality that shined like a jewel. She had a most expressive face and anyone could read like a book. Her eyes were always soft and never angry. She could do an inquisitive look when she had a question and even a mischievous look when she was acting that way.

I remember a time when I was putting a saddle on her to exercise her in the arena. First you put on a saddle blanket or pad, and then you put the saddle on top of that. I had put the blanket on and turned around to pick up the saddle. When I turned back around, the blanket was on the ground. I figured that I must have been mistaken in thinking I had centered it and that it had simply fallen off. So I set the saddle back where it was and once again placed the blanket on her back. I retrieved the saddle, only to turn and find the blanket on the ground once again.

I looked at Pearl, and I swear her eyes made her look like she was grinning impishly at me. When I saw the look, I knew she was playing with me. I went through the routine once again, only this time I faked picking the saddle up and turned back quickly to see her shaking her back to make the blanket fall to the ground. The look on her face turned from an impish grin to the startled look a child would give when caught with a hand in the cookie jar after being told they couldn't have any cookies. I was learning her and she was learning me. One thing was for sure, this was going to be fun, that much I could already tell.

Just as Bob's horse Double Bid was his favorite riding horse, Pearl rapidly became mine. I suppose her personality was one of those things passed on genetically from mother to daughter. That would be a good scientific explanation, but I prefer the idea that we were just both where we were supposed to be, doing what we were supposed to be doing. In all the years Pearl was here at the farm, she never had a bad day. Maybe I should say she never acted like she was having a bad day.

She was always ready for whatever we wanted her to do and never complained. She had several other jobs aside from being my personal riding horse. She was a riding lesson horse, and she was used to help give people who feared horses the tools to conquer their fear. She was semi-dominate in the herd, second only to Annie, and she had babies. She stayed busy with all her jobs and was always willing when we asked her to do even more. She loved attention. Whether it was a simple conversation or a complete grooming, she reacted like you had given her a bag of carrots all to herself.

I vividly remember one early fall day when I rode Pearl for the first time without reins. Until that day, I had never completely trusted any horse enough to ride in that manner and always rode with some sort of control. I was sitting on the wooden fence surrounding her pasture, and she joined me as she would often do. I was talking to her about many things, and as was usually the case during these conversations, she was standing with her head relaxed and lowered, listening to my voice. The subject matter of the conversation wasn't important; it was simply a chance to spend time together.

She was standing parallel to the fence at the time. I am not sure what came over me, but I gently slid off the fence and onto her back. She never even tensed but seemed to await a cue so she would know what I wanted her to do. I leaned back a little and squeezed with my legs, and we walked off. The two of us traveled around the pasture at a walk, turning as I cued her with my legs and stopping when I leaned back a little. I guided her back to the fence and stopped her where the walk had begun. I dismounted the same way I got on, by getting off her back and remounting the fence. She looked at me as if to say, "See, that wasn't so hard. You should have tried sooner." I bid her adieu and watched her watch me as I left the barn lot. Soon, she went back to doing what horses do, which is generally whatever they want. It's not really about getting a horse to do what you want; it is about getting them to agree to do what you want. Lesson learned.

Pearl had three foals while she was with us, and all of them had great conformation and attitudes. One of those foals was unplanned and was the result of what you might call an "oops moment." After Pearl's last "planned" foal was weaned, we decided to leave her open (or un-bred) because she was such a good riding horse, and we didn't want to limit time with her. Pearl was just good at everything you asked her to do.

We do not usually keep stud horses at this farm, but we had one here at the time that was almost two years old. His name was Smokey, and his dam was Annie. He was still here because he had cut his leg on the wire fence and was in the process of healing. He was also still in training. We kept him in a round pen adjacent to a stall so he wouldn't be close to the mares, and because it was easier to doctor him in that area and control the healing.

One morning, very early, I put Pearl in a lot in front of the barn before heading to town to run errands. I should have told Jennifer about moving Pearl but actually thought nothing of it. While I was gone, she let Smokey out of the round pen so he could get a little grass during the early part of the day. She didn't know Pearl was close by, nor did she know Pearl was in cycle for breeding. I returned home to find Jennifer trying desperately to get Smokey back in the pen and both horses trying just as desperately to tear the fence down so they could consummate their budding relationship.

A good average weight for a Quarter Horse is around one thousand pounds. Neither Jennifer nor I could convince these two large animals to stay apart. Since it was going to happen anyway, I just opened the gate to the pasture and let nature runs its intended course. The end result was one last foal for Pearl and a cigar for Smokey! Smokey went on to have a career as a cutting horse, working cattle in Kansas feed lot country. His life is a story in itself to be told another day. Pearl's days as a brood mare on our ranch ended with the birth of the unplanned foal, and the foaling was not without its drama and danger to her health.

I never watched Pearl have a foal during her three deliveries; she always did it by herself and apparently did it well. In this case, as with the other two, she had the foal alone, and that part went well. However, there was a problem that arose a few days later that could have cost her life.

About a week or ten days after foaling, we had some visitors at the farm who were looking at that year's crop of foals. I had noticed earlier that Pearl was acting a little off and was not her usual sociable self. She was keeping her foal away from people, when she was generally happy to have her offspring mix with humans and other beings. Her head was also down quite a bit, and she almost always held it up with her soft eyes showing curiosity about everything around her.

Just as I walked into the barn lot to check on her, she laid down with a thump, let out a big sigh, and called to her foal with a low rumbling call that mares use only with their foals. I had a strange feeling that I knew what the problem was, so I lifted her tail and took a quick look. Sure enough, she was leaking blood from her vagina. I had checked her the day she foaled, and I knew she hadn't torn herself. From my experience that left one possibility, although I am sure a real veterinarian could have cited many others. I felt she probably had an infection from not cleaning out after the birth.

When a mare has a foal, there is a long checklist of things you have to do and watch for, from giving tetanus shots to both of them to making sure the foal nurses and has a bowel movement. In the middle of the list of gotta-do's is the need to lay the placenta or birth sack out, inspect it, and make sure it is all there. We refer to the process of the mare expelling the placenta as "cleaning out," and it generally happens as nature intends it to. The problem is that if you are not there and the mare cleans out before you get to the placenta, they will walk on it and tear it with their hooves.

This is exactly what Pearl did. I checked the birth sack as closely as I could, but the torn state it was in did not make it possible for me to be sure it was all there. Pearl had always cleaned out before, so I assumed she had this time too. On that particular day, I had been around Pearl and the foal all morning, and she had acted like she was high on life. I guess you could say she acted the same way as she had after she foaled, and she didn't give me a hint anything was going on until it was almost too late.

We called the emergency into the veterinarian and awaited his arrival. I stayed beside the mare I had grown so very close to. Her respirations were rapid, and she never did get up. She let her foal nurse as she lay there waiting for some help for a problem I couldn't fix. I have found out during other similar experiences in my life that I do not like the feeling of being powerless. All I could offer was comfort and a calming presence. The vet knew I wouldn't have called unless the situation was serious, and he arrived quickly.

We managed to get Pearl up onto her feet. He had to run his hand inside her uterus and clean out the inner walls of any debris. The process is very uncomfortable for a horse, as you can imagine, and Pearl was no exception. As with everything else in her life, she stood still and did what was asked of her. After being cleaned out, she required a watchful eye for the next few days and a weeklong round of antibiotic shots, which would be administered by me.

Within a few short days, Pearl was back to normal, and the infection cleared up. I have owned a lot of horses in my life, and you have read about several in this book. I was connected to Pearl much like I was to a horse that came along later named Buffy. But where Buffy belonged to another person and I was truly her keeper, Pearl and I owned each other and were connected deeply in the life we led. I cringed inside when I thought of the possibility that I could have lost her. Little did I know that was exactly what was about to happen.

Living with the Choices You Make

Late in 2005, I started experiencing some rather disturbing and very painful symptoms that were limiting my mobility. The problem seemed to be centered around the middle of my back. I began receiving treatment for the pain, which consisted of shots in the spine. X-rays indicated I had a dire problem in my back. The origin of the problem was thought to be a rough life with a lot of bumps and bruises along the way and a little arthritis thrown in for good measure. Little did I know at the time that I was but a little over three years away from receiving a life-changing diagnosis that would tax me as no other would. During medical treatments and appointments, doctors told me my days of riding a horse and wrestling young weanlings needed to stop completely. They said one wrong fall from a horse—or anything else for that matter—could result in paralysis from the chest area down. Without personally experiencing the kind of love I have for this life I lead, you cannot have any idea how devastating this news was or how bad its effect was on my very being. What I perceived myself to be would be no longer. Changes were coming, whether I wanted them to or not. Choices would have to be made and the consequences of those choices lived with as I continued on in some fashion or another.

One thing I have learned without a doubt is life is cyclic. It is that way with the horse business part of what I do as well as with numerous other branches of daily existence; what comes around once will come around once again. What I had seen happen to others as they traveled a similar path might well come to pass in my own life, and I would have to work my way through that.

If you will remember, due to his advancing age and medical limitations, Bob Heady had to make the decision to give up his favorite horse or make an outstanding horse a pasture pet. Was he to keep his horse just for petting and looking at, feeding and grooming, loving and talking to, or would he offer her a better life with someone else? You obviously know what he chose to do from reading this far. Now I was facing the same dilemma with the daughter of his horse.

If I were to believe what I was being told by those trained to know, my riding days were over. I had on the farm a very special horse that deserved more of a life than I could possibly offer given the circumstances I faced. It became one of those things you know you have to do, but you make excuses constantly in order to keep from doing it. I fought making a decision for months, not days, constantly waffling back and forth and always finding a reason to leave things as they were.

The intuitive feelings that had been so strong in me took over and made me see I needed to make a decision based upon what was good for Pearl and not what I felt was good for me. I needed to allow her to have the possibility of a great life with someone else, and that someone else needed to be away from this area in order for the transition to work. Distance had to be part of the equation in order for me to stay away from her and let her acclimate to a new family. I had to let the universe work the same way it worked when she came here to live, which I believed was not a coincidence but something much greater. I needed to have an unwavering faith in what was supposed to be would be and all would turn out all right.

I had developed the habit of selling horses through a trusted auction site named Western Kentucky Horse Sales located in Bowling Green, Kentucky. There are many other auction businesses for horses, but I found the clientele at this particular location to be a little more informed about horses and what they were searching for in a horse. Many of the horses I have sold through this horse sale have also had the secondary benefit of allowing me to develop lifelong friendships with the buyers. I have had numerous calls from buyers long after a sale who just wanted to let me know how happy they were with their horse and how it was doing with its new life.

Western Kentucky Horse Sales had a sale coming up on March 25, 2006. The decision had been made, we would sell three horses at the sale to lighten the load around the farm and one of those would be my much loved Pearl. We all make choices in life, and those choices have a ripple effect that spreads throughout the universe. It was yet to be determined what future was created by the decision, but once it was made, we had to live with it. It is at this point I am reminded of a quote by Richard Bach, the author of *Jonathon Livingston Seagull,* who wrote, "Some choices we live not only once but a thousand times over, remembering them for the rest of our lives." And that has been the case with the decision we made to sell Pearl.

More rapidly than I could have imagined, the night before the sale date arrived. The gentleman who hauls horses for us always goes to the sale the night before, so he arrived at the farm the afternoon before the sale to load the horses and start his trip. I tried to keep my emotions in check and act in a businesslike manner but failed miserably. This was a horse that I was tied to emotionally and there I stood, willingly allowing her to depart. Unless you have experienced a situation like this, you can't imagine the speed with which you can change your mind over and over again. With a final caress, a spoken "Good-bye old friend," and a loving word of encouragement, Pearl was loaded on the trailer to set off toward the next destination in her life. It was hard to decipher her expression on that day, even though it had always been so easy in all our previous times together. The emotional part of me wanted to think she was let down at what she knew was happening. The now-muted logical part of me wondered if she might think she was just headed on another trail ride.

Personally, I knew what I was giving up. To me, a human's relationship with horses represents the wild part of our very being that is still genetically hardwired inside our psyche, while at the same time they supply the needed link to absolute freedom we secretly seek every day. This horse was my connection to that world of freedom, and this particular horse and I had a connection that fit perfectly. As I watched the trailer pull out of the barn drive, I was devastated and overwhelmed with feelings of loss and confusion. I walked away with my head low and my mind spinning with conflicting emotions.

I found myself questioning my decision again the next day when I received word Pearl had sold for a much lower price than she should have brought. We had a girl who was supposed to ride Pearl through the ring and show how well trained she was, but that wasn't what happened. The young lady's mother insisted the girl wear a helmet during the ride, and the handler thought that would send the wrong message to the potential buyers, a message that the horse could be hard to handle or dangerous. So he made the decision to lead her through the ring instead of riding her himself. The end result was that people were bidding on word alone without any proof.

Had Pearl been allowed to show how good she was, the bidding would have been more brisk and the odds of her going to knowledgeable horse people would have been much greater. I had to remind myself that money was not the reason for selling Pearl. Putting her future in the hands of a good family trumped money, and time would tell if this goal had been accomplished successfully. It would not be long before I would begin to search in earnest for Pearl's new home so that I could see firsthand if she had found a good one.

A Change of Name

Life continued on, just as life tends to do, regardless of what swirls around in our minds. When you run horse stables, it is a daily job without let up, so it wasn't difficult to find things to keep me physically busy and my mind occupied. Regardless of the workload, thoughts of Pearl and worries about her safety gnawed at me constantly. I took my stewardship very seriously, and until I knew for sure that she was okay, I just couldn't let things lie. Even though ownership had changed hands, a self-assigned onus was on me to make sure Pearl was having a good life.

A few months after the sale, due to my constant worrying about whether or not I had made the right choice, I decided to try and locate Pearl's buyers. All I had to go on was the names James and Shelia Puckett and the state of Illinois. Since I had been an investigator prior to owning horse stables, I felt that was enough information to go on. The search began in earnest to locate them and was fueled by the nagging need to be reassured that the right connection had been made. It would have been easier if that was all I was looking for, but just to cloud things up a little, I had decided I also wanted to purchase her back from her new owners and return her home. See, with me the waffling never ceased. The longer the separation, the more I missed her and wanted her back if at all possible.

In order to make a very long search a short story, I finally located the Pucketts in Carbondale. As the final step of the search, I was able to make contact with someone who knew them. They said they would call the Pucketts, let them know who I was, and provide them with my number if they chose to call me. Remember the quote about all choices change the future? Well, here is another example that verifies the truthfulness of that ism. Sheila Puckett called me the next day, and a long-distance friendship with the family began. Sheila works at the Southern Illinois University at Carbondale. She manages the school's horse farm breeding, foal watch, riding horses, and research programs, as well as some teaching labs at the horse center. Additionally, she and her husband Jimmy manage their own farm horse breeding program and marketing. If that sounds like a full plate, it is.

Sheila related to me that "Kate" (now called by her given name rather than the name Matt gave her) was working at the college too. Because of her gentle temperament and the abilities she had due to her training, she was being used in the beginning riders program for people who had little history with horses or a little fear of them. Sheila also told me they loved her and couldn't believe what a bargain they got when they purchased her. And no, they had no intention of selling her, but if they ever decided to, I would be the first person they would call.

I was dejected because I had been turned down regarding a possible purchase, yet at the same time I was elated that Pearl had found what sounded like the perfect home. Well, other than the perfect home here where I wanted her taking up residence once again. At her new home, she had a purpose, which she had always wanted, and people who knew horses to care for her. I suppose the effects of my choice were evident in the good life and promising future she had with the Puckett family. We ended our conversation with promises to stay in touch.

Over the years to come, I called occasionally and renewed my offer to buy Pearl back, but Jimmy and Sheila were steadfast in their dedication to this mare. She was part of their family and would remain so. I remember one time when, perhaps growing a wee bit tired of my repeated attempts to buy her, Jimmy said okay and shot me a price that was quite high. I saw through the offer and decided I should just remain friendly and let Pearl have her life in Illinois . . . or did I?

On December 14, 2011, facing some major health challenges that I found quite taxing, I decided once more to attempt to buy Pearl back. I called and spoke to Sheila and told her what was going on in my life and how I would once more like to offer to buy Pearl so I could have some time with her. The decision to share this information with Sheila was tremendously difficult to reach because I had only shared this personal information with a handful of people. We talked on the phone that day for a very long time, but the answer was still no, Pearl (Kate) couldn't be purchased.

Unknown to me, for the past six years Pearl had been Jimmy and Sheila's daughter Katie's main riding horse. Katie had been showing her, and her ownership had been officially changed into Katie's name. Sheila went on to relay several stories about the relationship between daughter and horse that I found quite touching. We talked about sharing pictures and during the conversation found out we both were using Facebook. With promises to "friend" each other on the site, we ended the conversation. I couldn't wait to see pictures of my old friend once again and read about her new life.

What I saw after we allowed each other access to our profiles was much more than pictures. After viewing the relationship and love Katie and Kate exhibited when they were together, something changed inside me and brought me the peace I needed. It is difficult to explain, but I will try. If you will notice, I referred to Pearl as Kate in the previous sentence for the first time. I mentioned the name Kate, but I personally referred to her as Pearl. After seeing the magic shared by the two of them, she became Kate in my eyes. She was now Kate who belonged to a little girl in Carbondale, Illinois, named Katie. No longer was she Pearl who belonged in Kentucky.

After seeing how special they were together, I knew I could never play any part in separating the two of them. I saw how shallow I was being with my continued pursuit to satisfy my needs over anyone else's. I was able to let things go and let them be with the knowledge that the effects of my choice were good effects. The future my choice created was an exceptional future for this family and for Kate. Jimmy and Sheila's choice to buy Kate created magical effects in their life as well. Things are as they are supposed to be. As you will see, coincidence played no part in this story, none at all.

Katie and Kate "Eventing." Courtesy of Sheila Puckett

One Last Call

In 2010, while in the midst of writing this book, I decided this story should be a part of the book because of all the oddities that had occurred which I considered serendipitous in nature and certainly not coincidental. When I decided to write the story, I still had hopes a homecoming for Kate would not only be good for me, but somewhere in the recesses of my mind I thought it would also be a great ending for the saga we experienced together. As things turned out, the ending of the story is even better than I ever could have imagined. It's funny how things turn out that way if you just let them and quit fighting the nature of things. Even with all I had going on in my life, I still had the potential to learn, grow, and let little occurrences like this take my mind off of anything troubling me. Growth, wonder, hope, and faith are the things I gained from this whole experience.

After seeing the pictures of Kate and Katie, I wanted to have at least one more lengthy conversation with Sheila and Katie. There were a few answers I still needed in order to stitch the complete story together. Without letting them know the direction I was headed, I considered it necessary to find out if their initial contact with Kate was serendipitous or simply synchronous in nature. We made arrangements to have a phone conversation between the three of us and discuss the day of the sale when they bought Kate and a little about their life together.

After pleasantries and small talk, I asked Sheila, "What made you decide to bid on Kate at the auction, and when was the first time you saw her?"

Sheila replied, "We don't go to that auction very often. We were going to look at a horse that was for sale, potentially to buy it for someone else. We had no intentions of buying a horse for us. The first time we saw her was when she was led into the sale ring." She said that she and Jimmy thought it odd that she was being led through the ring instead of being ridden and couldn't believe how low the bids were. It ended up being a last-second decision to bid on Kate. The fact that they bought another horse was a complete surprise to the both of them.

They took Kate home to Illinois, and Jimmy rode her right away. They could not believe how well-trained and compliant to cues she was, especially if you took into account it was her first day at a new place and with new people. Kate's new life began that day as a member of the Puckett family.

One of the first things they noticed was how easy to read Kate's facial expressions were when they were around her and how intuitive Kate was to Katie's mood. Their whole relationship took on the air of seemingly being quite "spiritual" in nature. We discussed the commonality we shared in experiencing Kate's ability to communicate by using her eyes. Sheila shared one story about Kate where she was on a trailer and her lead became unhooked. She was happily munching hay that had fallen on the floor of the trailer when Katie noticed she was unhooked during a stop and called to her. Kate raised her head up and appeared to be delighted to see Katie, seemed to smile at the recognition, and as was her nature, exhibited happiness for the human contact. However, after Katie hooked her back up and she could no longer get to the hay below, Kate pinned her ears back and glared at Katie as if to demandingly say, "Unhook me right now. I was eating." Shelia said Kate could communicate frustration, glee, mischief, love, and downright happiness with her eyes.

They also told me that Kate was a very loving and protective horse. She loved foals and got along with goats and donkeys too. Sheila said, "We used to have chickens, but something got into the chicken coop one night and killed all of the chickens but one. We decided to just turn it loose, because we felt it was safer outside than back in the coop. Every evening around dusk, the chicken would make its way to its favorite roosting place on Kate's back, and there it would roost all night. The chicken felt it was a safe place, and Kate let it stay there."

When I was first given the ability to access pictures the Puckett family had taken over the years, I saw one that completely surprised me. The picture was of Kate jumping an obstacle on a course while being ridden by Katie. The look of determination on both of their faces was extremely evident. During Kate's time in my life, she was strictly a Western-style horse, and jumping with her in that style of riding never crossed my mind.

I asked Sheila about the picture and she said, "Katie was showing Eventing [a horse riding discipline], and we had a finished jumper for her to compete with, but it got sick and couldn't compete anymore. We bought her another well-trained horse, and it came down with colic, had surgery, and died. For a while we were without a trained horse for Katie to compete on. We discovered by accident that Kate could jump. The first two times she was asked to jump, she did so without hesitation. She just naturally became Katie's competition horse and did quite well."

This was another of those familiar stories within a story when you are writing about things being meant to be or things happening as they are supposed to. Throughout my time with Kate, she always did what you asked her to do and did it well. There was always a possibility she might not like it, but she never failed to give it the best she could.

A determined Kate and Katie jumping! Courtesy of Sheila Puckett

Kate is eighteen years old now and has had one foal since she arrived at the Puckett farm. It is a yearling stud colt with Kate's personality. Their plans for her future are close to a semi-retirement for a horse like Kate. She will have a few more babies and be ridden on a regular basis. She will remain Katie's horse, because as Sheila said, "They bonded early and have a special relationship. They are a team and a partnership." In a note that Katie wrote to me about her relationship with Kate, she ended it with the following:

She will forever be my Kate, my true and faithful partner. Little did we know that day that Mom and Jimmy bought her, she would change my life forever and become such an intricate piece in my life's puzzle. She was the missing link that completed me.

If I could give Kate one more message, it would be to tell her that no matter how much I miss her being in my life, no matter how much I love her or how much I enjoyed the magical time we shared, I have finally and thankfully reached a point where I can truthfully say I am glad I made the choice to let her go and find the happiness she lives with every day of her life. I am glad that during the day of the sale, she was led through the ring and not ridden or allowed to show what she was trained to do. If she had, the bidding would have been much higher, and she might not have found her way to the Puckett home. I am glad she did not stay here just for me to look at and talk to. I am glad she found the purpose she needed. I am happy the effects of my choice were for her and Katie to find each other through the power of this universe and develop the special bond that they have. I am glad she has had a wonderful life with the Puckett family and lives in a forever home. Without the choice being made, the effects never happen, and a chance for real growth and positive change are stymied.

As this tale winds to an end, I am reminded of a quote that has been passed around the horse world for many years. The author is unknown, so I cannot give credit where it is certainly due. It goes like this: "All horses deserve, at least once in their lives, to be loved by a little girl." How appropriate the words, how deserving the horse, how lucky the girl! All things happen as they are supposed to; just learn to let them. Have I learned? Let's just say I am successfully advancing from level to level with hopes of graduating on time. Now for the question, was it serendipity or synchronicity? Coincidence or no such thing? I suppose the answer is up to the reader. I know what I believe.

Chapter Nine

Cookie and the Coon

Everyone has to make their own decisions. I still believe that. You just have to be able to accept the consequences without complaining.
—Grace Jones

L IFE ON OUR HORSE FARM is generally quiet and serene. We are blessed to live on a little gem of land that sits within the boundaries of three of the largest grain farmers in this county. It is a peaceful existence being surrounded by corn, soybeans, tobacco, and wheat during the growing season or fallow ground in the winter. The crops can lull you to sleep as the wind travels through their leaves and whispers goodnight after the moon has made its nightly, shape-shifting appearance.

There just isn't a lot of traffic on our road or other noise out our way like the din most people have become accustomed to hearing. Oh, we have migrating birds like Sandhill cranes or Canada geese honking their songs as they travel through, or the occasional howling and yipping of coyotes hunting in packs after some helpless prey. Otherwise, the quiet contains a peacefulness most people would love to experience. I'm sure there are people who love the noise and hustle of the city, but we are not among them. We seem to thrive on the peace and tranquility of farm life.

During one recent winter night, we found that peacefulness violated by the barking of our dog Cookie. Cookie is definitely a little ankle nipper and very protective of our family. I do not know if this protectiveness comes from a feeling of indebtedness because she feels she won the lottery when we adopted her from the local pound and needs to repay us, or if some part of her DNA just requires it because of her genetic heritage. Either way, she loves us and distrusts most of the other beings that come this way.

Cookie is normally a very quiet little dog, so much so we thought her mute for the longest time. In hindsight, maybe she just didn't have anything to bark about, because most people would stay in their cars and wait for us to come outside and keep a certain little puffed-up fur ball away from them. Little she is, weighing in at around thirty pounds. But when she puffs up, she looks much bigger, and her bright white teeth stand out in stark contrast to her black fur-covered body. Once we are outside, she leaves people alone . . . mostly.

Cookie came to us after our longtime farm dog Sarge died of cancer at the age of eleven. Now Sarge was a lover of anyone who petted him. I swear that golden retriever would help you pack away anything you wanted to relieve us of having ownership in as long as you petted him or fed him a treat. He would bark at varmints during the night, but once they paid heed to his orders to leave, he would quiet down and go back to bed. There were very few nights where I had to get up and go to the door to quiet him down so we could sleep.

With Cookie, her muteness was a gift we all enjoyed. We wanted a dog that would keep the varmints away and one that would leave the cats alone. We hit a home run with both of those wishes. She would quietly chase varmints but yet share her doghouse with the two barn cats that always migrated to the house at night. She loves those cats and I guess sees them as part of the herd she is entrusted to care for.

So I was completely shocked when she woke us up one Saturday night during the dead of winter with a steady, irritating, high-pitched barking that would not stop.

≈

One of the steadfast rules concerning life in the country is you don't holler at your dogs when they are barking in the middle of the night. After all, that is why you have them. You want their bark to chase off animals or people that you don't want around. It's not like we have nearby neighbors who will be offended by a barking dog. My motto is to let dogs be and let them do their job. Cookie's barking would chase the offender away soon enough, and all would go back to being peaceful. That was my thinking, anyway.

The barking that night was incessant and sleep was impossible. Cookie howled on and on, seemingly without a breath. There were brief moments of silence, but apparently it was so her vocal cords could recharge. Then the barking would start again, generally just about the time I was drifting back to sleep once more. I covered my head with the pillow, put my fingers in my ears, and attempted to meditate my way past the noise. Nothing was working. After about an hour and a half, I decided to go outside with a flashlight and see if I could find out what was keeping Cookie barking and me awake.

I found Cookie very alert and on edge. She was not puffed up like she gets with strangers; she just gave the impression of a very busy dog with an important job to accomplish. Still, she came to me when I exited the house and stood by my side as I scanned the yard for whatever had caused the problem. I looked everywhere, including the woodpile and the two trees behind the house, and was unable to find anything. Yet Cookie remained by my side, visibly upset by something. I petted her and thanked her for doing a good job and went back to bed.

I had high hopes of returning to sleep, but the din started anew about the time my head hit the pillow. I knew there wasn't a prowler hanging about with the intention of harming my family, because I had just looked around with that in mind. Nor did I see any lions or tigers hiding behind trees waiting to pounce on any unsuspecting prey. So I did what any sane, knowledgeable, and understanding person would do: I went and yelled at the dog to shut up. Now, Cookie is a very tender-hearted little dog, and I am sure I had just hurt her feelings, and I really did feel bad for doing it, but I (selfishly) wanted to go to sleep. She tucked her tail between her legs and crawled into her doghouse. The two barn cats, apparently thinking they were next, went in with her. I went guiltily back to bed and slept fitfully the rest of the night.

The next morning, very early the next morning, the barking started once again. Cookie waited until she heard people moving about for the day, and she went back to work. I was dressed, so I grabbed the flashlight once again and went outside. This time I was kinder to the dog than I had been during our last encounter, and I did a better scan of the area. It didn't hurt the odds of a successful search when Cookie ran to one of the trees out back and looked up at it while barking. Finally, I saw the object of her attention; she had treed a raccoon the night before and it was still in the crook of the tree, apparently feeling it was hidden and out of reach.

Varmints are part of life on any farm. Raccoons are feed stealers extraordinaire and will, when cornered, attempt to hurt the being that put them in such a position. It is a constant battle to keep them out of the feed room. Once they gain entrance, they can open most feed containers and eat their fill, ensuring their eventual return. We live trap them quite often and relocate them to other farms in the vicinity. I know, not very neighborly, but it rids us of the problem until the other farmers live trap them and bring them back. I do generally relocate them to areas rich in an environment suited to raccoons; those environments just happen to be close to other farms.

We also get our share of other animals seeking shelter and food. Opossums are a constant threat, and they carry a disease in their feces that is deadly to horses. People are always dropping off cats that then seek a handout. The problem is we can only have so many cats, and we don't want any opossums or raccoons, so we live trap and relocate. In the case of cats, they have to go to shelters like the one where ours came from, even though it may seem harsh. We cannot take in every stray that is dropped off for us, and people shouldn't expect us to. Our hearts are huge, but our pocketbook is limited. We do what we can.

So we had a terrified raccoon trapped up a tree, a barking dog wanting to make sure it stayed right there, two curious barn cats that were eager to watch the show, and one farm owner who felt like he had to do something because that is what men do. That is not to brag and say what we do is always the right thing, because unfortunately most of you know that isn't true. But we always feel some action is called for, and it is up to us to come up with a plan for such action.

I went back into the house to sip my morning coffee and think about what I could do to make sure everyone came out of this uninjured and the offending, trespassing raccoon would leave, scared so badly it would never entertain the thought of returning. I would like to say that my wife Jennifer looked upon me lovingly as I sat there and taxed my mind for solutions to this family dilemma. But truth be told, I think she looked at me with a great amount of incredulity and a hint of exasperation. Trust me, you can't mistake the two looks. She knew from experience that once again I would not leave well enough alone and allow Mother Nature to work her magic. No, I would once again interfere out of some misguided male-ego-driven sense that I had to fix the problem. I plead guilty to all past problem-solving debacles I have been a part of, but I was convinced this time things would be different.

The first attempt to dislodge the raccoon from its place of safety came from me. I had the bright idea if I poked him in the butt with a stick, he would run out of the tree and away from us, never to return. Well, it didn't exactly happen the way I had planned. I had a long stick that barely reached him, and I gave him a good poke, hoping for the best. What happened instead was the coon scurried farther up the tree, out of reach from the stick and from me. The second thing I tried was to have Matt, our son, get the .22-caliber pistol and load it with birdshot. The intent was to shoot the gun into the air. We were hoping the loud noise would scare the raccoon off without harming him, but that didn't work either. As a matter of fact, he ran even farther away, managing to make it to the small limbs at the end of the branch, where he sat swaying in the breeze and staring at me.

During the third attempt, I stood at the bottom of the tree and threw small sticks at him, once again hoping for the best. This is where he did the funniest thing, causing me to go to the house for the camera in the hope I could get a picture of him doing it again. While watching me throw sticks at him, he covered his eyes with one of his paws. I guess he was saying, "If I can't see you then you can't see me." This was coming from a raccoon that, even though not an adult, still weighed eighteen to twenty pounds and couldn't possibly be missed as he clung to branches about the size of a pencil while up in a winter tree with no leaves. It was so funny and endearing that I started looking at him in quite a different light. As I look back, I wish I had heeded the message Mother Nature sent me and stopped all attempts to get him to leave. It pains me to admit I didn't listen.

≈

©2013 Jess Parker-Andrews Art & Illustration

It was around this time that my wife and son had to leave for school. Both are attending the local college, one intending to teach and the other to further her nutritional education. I was admonished by both of them to leave the raccoon alone until they returned or, better yet, just leave it alone completely with the hope it would leave when no one was looking.

Now, I have a question. If under such circumstances I acknowledged them with a nod or the word okay, does it make me a liar if I had no intention of leaving the raccoon alone? Before you answer, keep in mind they knew from experience that I wouldn't abide with the restrictions placed upon me by the two of them. They know me and know I would say whatever it took to get them safely off to school without fear of me being injured. I didn't want their minds occupied with such thoughts when they should be learning and enjoying their higher education experience. Well, that was my justification for the nod and the assurance that I would leave the animal alone, fully knowing I was about to do something to ensure the animal would be gone by the time they returned. Or so I thought. As soon as the dust cleared the driveway and they were no longer in sight, I got busy formulating plan number four.

I have a twelve-foot stepladder in the shop and a telescoping pole I use to prune high branches out of trees. I figured that if I put the ladder under the tree and used the end of the pole without the saw, I could convince the raccoon to leave the tree. I would be the hero and would be able to tell everyone (while sipping a beer and expanding my chest) how I managed to convince him to leave. I originally thought it was a good idea—and it might have been if things had worked out as planned.

I figured it wouldn't do for Cookie to be under the tree when the raccoon decided to leave, so my first step was to put her on her cable. She immediately started barking at the raccoon, putting it a little on edge. I then got the ladder and pruning pole situated. This would probably be a good time to tell you that I was not supposed to be on ladders, wouldn't it? I had a back surgery in 2010 and have rods, plates, and screws in my T-spine. My mobility and balance are affected a little but not my want-to-do. It was still strong.

Well, I climbed about six and a half feet up the ladder and set about poking the raccoon with the pole. The limb started bouncing with his weight and the wind. I smiled, but only once. You see, when I first started poking, I thought this plan was going to be a good one after all. The smile faded quickly when I discovered I had not thought things completely through, nor had I prepared myself for any of the vast possible outcomes that could take place. The raccoon was indeed going to come out of the tree. The problem was that he was going to come straight down on me. I think I had been kind of hoping he would scurry down the same way he got up, but that didn't happen.

Instead, he lost his grip on the branches and fell right out of the tree, and I broke his fall. Trust me, this is not a position you want to find yourself in when you can't move with speed and agility and you are six and a half feet up in the air on a ladder you are not supposed to be standing on. I can only imagine the open-mouthed, gaping look of disbelief on my face as these events took place. The raccoon hit my shoulder and leg on his way to the ground, bounced once, and got his feet under him faster than I could react to the fact that he was no longer in the tree.

In his confusion and panic, he commenced to run circles around the ladder so fast I could barely see him in a blur of gray and black with just a hint of white for his teeth. All the while he was making a strange snarling sound. The dog had set up a barking frenzy that added to the noise. I believe I also heard something that sounded like a school child screaming like someone had thrown a spider down her blouse during recess. The noise I was hearing could have been me, but I was trying too hard not to pee in my pants to take the time to figure out where the noise was coming from.

I did know one thing: the raccoon wanted back in the tree, and I was between him and where he wanted to be. He couldn't go to the other side of me, because that would put him closer to the snarling dog. That only left him one choice—and up the ladder he went. It ended up being one of those days where I was glad I wear lined jeans in the winter. Up my right leg he went, then between my arms holding the ladder, and on up to the top. Once there, he sprang the remaining three feet to the tree while I leapt in slow motion the other way.

To add offence to an already insulting day, the ladder fell on top on me as I lay on the ground wondering exactly where I went wrong after getting out of bed that morning. My hearing has diminished with age, but I swear I heard a strange, high-pitched whimpering coming from somewhere!

The raccoon ended up right back where he started before I poked him and I belatedly decided that was a good place for him. His butt was turned towards me as if to once again say, "I can't see you, so you can't see me." Or it could have meant something else I guess, but let's not go there.

I gathered myself up, looked around to see if anyone had witnessed the event and then checked myself for injuries. My ego was badly damaged, but otherwise my pants were dry and apparently I was in good shape. No one but Cookie had seen what happened or heard the screaming, and although she looked like she was grinning, she at least couldn't tell the tale. Nor were there any rabies vaccinations in my near future. I decided to leave the raccoon alone as Mother Nature intended me to do all along. She had tried to tell me, but I wasn't listening. I cut Cookie loose, and she didn't pay any more attention to the raccoon the rest of the day. I returned to the house for some deep thinking.

As I sat at the kitchen table sipping a hot cup of coffee, well after the adrenaline rush had subsided, the apparently rusty wheels of reason in my mind started slowly turning. With deep gratitude for the true nature of the situation I had found myself caught up in, I came to the appreciative realization that I was the only one with knowledge of what had transpired. Furthermore, the truth could go to the grave with me. I need not be embarrassed, and my bruised ego could heal without sharing any of the events that happened earlier.

I decided I could tell my family upon their return I had in fact followed their advice and left the raccoon alone. I had the proof because the raccoon was still in the tree, exactly where he was when they left. Of course I would have to hide my grass-stained jeans in the laundry basket or, like poor old Lucy when Ricky Ricardo caught her stretching the truth, I would have some "splaining" to do.

In a painful rush of insight, I quickly came to the realization that my plan would not stand up to the test of reason my wife and son would put it through. I wouldn't be able to answer all their questions without sinking deeper yet into the pit of deceit. See, they know me better than anyone else, and they knew when they left that I would do something in an attempt to get the raccoon to leave. Regardless of my assurances to the contrary, they have been around me long enough to know I would try something. They had just hoped I wouldn't hurt myself in the process. Saying I didn't do anything but play on the computer and read the paper would not work.

Remembering the words of the immortal author and orator Mark Twain, who said, "If you tell the truth, you don't have to remember anything," I decided to tell it like it happened and take another hit to my already bruised ego. And that is exactly what I did. My wife just stared quietly as I told the story, slowly lowered her head, and shook it as she walked away, deep in her own thoughts and mumbling under her breath. Sometimes I feel sorry for the things I put her through. My son, although exhibiting a little more fire, realized that all was well and the world had not tilted during his absence. I had managed to do about what they expected of me, but I knew that after some time passed they would forgive me.

Oh, and the raccoon? He spent the day in the tree, sleeping on the small branches that were rocking with the wind. He never paid any mind to people, horses, or dogs. He showed his true nocturnal colors. Cookie paid him little attention the rest of the day. Sometime during the night, he left the confines of the tree and the farm. We haven't had a raccoon problem for quite a while now. I guess he shared the story with his family, and maybe they had a good laugh. It wouldn't surprise me if they watch from the distance to see if anything like that occurs again!

Me? I vowed to try to be a better listener when Mother Nature speaks to me. She wouldn't have to yell; I would try to catch the subtleties in her voice and heed the warnings . . . probably.

So, you might ask just how this story fits in with the theme of spirituality. The answer would be found in comparing the new me to the me of old. Had something like this happened not too many years ago, I would have taken great offense at the series of events that befell me that day. I would have screamed profanities. I would have taken all that happened personally, and I would have had one of the old-fashioned conniption fits I mentioned in previous stories. I would have wondered out loud what the Creator had against me. I would have been stuck in a "woe is me" mentality, and this feeling would have stayed with me throughout the day.

The new me? Well, he sees things in a different and more positive light. I didn't get hurt though I could have very easily. The dog and cats had a good laugh. The raccoon got safely away, and thankfully my wife and son were not here to witness my lesson being learned. That lesson was to just let things be as they are supposed to be. Allow the universe to work, and stop worrying about every possible chance of a negative outcome. For every negative possibility, there is a positive one that could just as easily occur. Put your energies to work on believing the best possible outcome will happen, and you might just be surprised how often it does.

Chapter Ten

Old Kate

Horses change lives. They give our young people
confidence and self esteem. They provide peace and
tranquility to troubled souls. They give us hope.
—Toni Robinson

S OME MAY SAY I WRITE a lot about the death of animals, but I prefer
to think I celebrate their lives by painting a picture of the way they
lived, their personalities, and some of the experiences we shared along
the way. So I start this story by saying, "Yes, a horse dies at the end."
But the story is much more than that. Is it an emotional story that
might make you cry? Maybe, but it will also make you smile because
this was one obstinate little mare who could be filled with love for you
one moment and the next moment the devil would take up residence
inside her and make her do things the complete opposite of being the
caring horse you were fooled into thinking she was.

Kate was a gift for my son Matt on Father's Day. I know it sounds a
bit strange, but I used to give him gifts on Father's Day as well as receive
them from him. I figured that without him, I wouldn't be celebrating
this hallmark day. Kate was purchased in Indiana during Matt's sixth
year and was his first horse. She was what is called a tri-colored Paint
mare. This means she was white, brown, and black, but mostly white.
She was probably around nineteen to twenty years old. The person who

had her for sale said she was nine years old, and I remember grinning real big. I guess he must have thought I looked a little inexperienced, but I was fairly good at aging a horse from its teeth. She was starting to show some arthritis in her left front leg, but otherwise she looked healthy. She was a brown-eyed beauty, and her looks certainly held your attention.

It was a stretch to actually call Kate a horse, and I do so only because of the size of her heart not her stature. Kate was only 13-3 hands high, just the size where she would be referred to as a cow pony or a cow horse. Because of her size, she was officially listed as a pony. Kate was 13 hands plus three fingers tall at the withers. To be a considered a horse, she would have had to be fourteen hands tall. However, her heart made her eighteen hands tall, and she would proudly let you know it. Most ponies are that way; they have what some people call "little person syndrome." They make up for their size with tons of attitude. I figured she was small enough for Matt to handle and large enough for me to ride for the occasional attitude adjustment. That ended up being a questionable belief on my part.

The day I introduced Kate to Matt was a nice day for the time of year, not too hot and a little breezy. You could see the surprise in his eyes as he accepted responsibility for her future. I saddled her up with the new saddle I had bought for the occasion, and Matt rode her that day around the barn lot. I led, given that Matt was a novice, but he did get to ride. I had a lot of fun watching this process, so much fun in fact that at the end of his ride, I decided I wanted to ride her too. Have you ever wished you could go back in time and change decisions you had made? This was one of those moments.

I should point out that I had had my forth knee surgery two days prior to Father's Day. Looking back on my decision to ride Kate that day, I can honestly say it wasn't a good idea. However, I didn't have the gift of hindsight at the moment, and I just loved riding horses. I couldn't get my leg high enough to get in the saddle, so I led her up beside a hay bunker. For those of you that do not know, a hay bunker is a v-shaped wooden piece with sides and legs that you can put a bale of hay in when you feed horses in a pasture. It is about two and one half feet tall and relatively sturdy. I made my way up onto the hay bunker and eased myself gently into the saddle. And then, as Matt says, "the rodeo ride started."

It is funny how things sometimes seem to happen in slow motion and you can remember each move that was made. I didn't much more than get my seat when Kate decided it was time to start the show. Apparently, she did not want a one-legged fat man on her back. I really don't consider myself fat, but I definitely weighed considerably more than a six-year-old boy. I guess she thought she had participated nicely in the pony show and let us take pictures, but now her day was over. I pulled her in, and she twisted out, she bowed her back, crow hopped, and squealed like a wounded pig. And believe it or not, in the background, I heard laughter. Yep, laughter! Since no one but my son and I were there, there was no question in my mind who was laughing.

Kate cut a quick spin to the right and unceremoniously dumped me on the ground. I couldn't hold on through that spin because I couldn't use both legs to grip her sides. And when she threw me, I landed right on the recently repaired leg. The knee of my jeans was soon soaked with blood. I didn't do what I wanted to do at the moment. Instead I gathered her up, got squarely in her face, and told her to remember that day, because we would have round two, and I would be ready for her. To be absolutely honest, that probably is not exactly what I said, but it's close enough for you to get what I meant. The laughter and smirking continued from her new fan, who apparently thoroughly enjoyed witnessing Kate and I putting on a show for his benefit.

And thus began my relationship with this hard-headed little horse who I grew to love and appreciate for being exactly what she was and no more. Our relationship would span almost seven years, and there never was a day I ever regretted bringing her into our family.

≈

Kate took to Matt and he took to her in quick order. They became inseparable. He would groom her and talk, and she would stand and listen. She got along with him just fine. She did not get along with other horses very well, and that is an understatement. She would boss, squeal, and try her best to be the dominant horse no matter where we put her or who we put her up against. I had to give it to her—she was full of try and possessed absolutely no give. She didn't always succeed in getting her way, but she was always in the thick of the mix every time. As I watched her attempts at being the boss or getting her way in matters, I secretly hoped my son would learn one lesson from her: to never quit trying to reach your goals.

Other than her arthritis, Kate seemed to be quite a healthy horse. The arthritis did become a problem later and limited her somewhat, but it never got her down, except maybe on farrier day. A farrier is a horse hoof specialist. They trim a horse's hooves much like we cut our fingernails. They do corrective trimming, and they shoe horses that need to be shod. A good farrier is a must for the serious horse owner.

Kate's knee hurt so badly at times that she would have to lie on the ground to have her feet trimmed. A horse has to have a lot of trust to do that, and Kate did become trusting. Eventually Ron Bryson, our farrier, developed a way to trim her without lifting her feet too high, and because Kate trusted him, she would stand for the trimming. His method did require him to practically stand on his head, but he never seemed to mind. That was one of the things I like about Ron; his love for horses trumped his need for money. He could have just as easily said he couldn't trim Kate and gone about his business, but instead he devised a method that worked. As a result, the trust flowed both ways. Maybe that is a lesson we should all learn.

Matt's relationship with Kate took a temporary step backwards one beautiful fall day. We had some friends out for the day, and everyone had been riding horses and having fun. Matt had been riding Kate, and all was going well. The day was winding down on a good note for everybody. We had taken the saddle and other tack off Kate when Matt said he wanted to ride her bareback. I tried to dissuade him from doing that, because he had never ridden bareback before. This fact was a failure on my part. I used to give lessons and always had the riders start off bareback in order to learn balance. Matt had learned to hang on and ride but not how to balance. In the famous last words of many before me, I said, "What the heck, go ahead."

It turned out to be another of those days where Kate had decided her day was over; she had played her part well, but that particular pony show had ended. Matt got on her, but she wouldn't do anything. She just stood there with the defiant look in her eye that I had grown accustomed to seeing. So what was a good father to do? I smacked Kate on the butt, and off she went galloping into the sunset with the boy hanging on for dear life. Not knowing how to balance, Matt started listing to starboard, slid off, hit the ground, and bounced at least three times by my count. I stood there with my mouth agape, emotions flooding over with feelings of guilt, like most good fathers would.

I picked Matt up, dried his tears, caught Kate, and made Matt mount back up. This was no small feat but was something that has to be done after a fall. Afterwards I had Jodi, a good friend who was there for the day, ride the wheels off the little mare to teach her that the day wasn't over until we said the day was over. Jodi got the duty that day because, even under the circumstances, I didn't want Kate carrying my extra weight on her knee. Kate learned her lesson that afternoon, and we didn't have any more problems—at least during riding sessions. Oh, we had occasional problems, but never while riding or handling her.

I think Kate learned something that day: her actions could hurt someone dear to her. The pecking order had been established. Matt was the boss, and Jennifer, my wife with the big heart for misunderstood animals, was second. Me? Well I stood somewhere out in right field doing pirouettes and picking at blades of grass. At least I was acknowledged and in the picture. And by the way, I did get round two in by riding Kate at a later date. Surprisingly, we did not have a problem. I would like to think she knew I was fully healed and didn't want to test me. But for all I knew, she could have taken pity on me and just didn't want to hurt or embarrass me again. You never knew with Kate.

≈

I guess a truce of sorts was reached that day because we never had another issue when it was time for Kate to work, ride, or be tended to by farriers or veterinarians. She was always compliant. She would still get that look in her eye, but she never followed through. Her relationship with Matt deepened and grew. She turned out to be the horse I had hoped for when I brought her home.

Now, I never said the same truce she had with us applied to other horses, dogs, cats, or birds. Kate would pin her ears back and squeal at anything moving if it violated her space. Kate's space included wherever she could see. She would chase all of the above mentioned animals with an angry eye if they provoked her by coming too close or sometimes just for looking at her. I remember one time she chased a full-size coyote that was on the other side of the fence, well away from her but close enough for her to feel her space intruded upon. She reminded me of a blue jay directing traffic at a bird feeder, letting the others know when they had had enough to eat or when they should leave. If there ever was a Napoleonic little horse, it was Kate. Fortunately, it was only other animals that caught the wrath of Kate and not humans. With us, she became what is known as an easy keeper.

I have often written about horse personalities and am convinced each and every one of them has their own unique traits. Some of my loyal readers will know my feelings concerning horses (and other animals) and know that I believe each one is different. They possess gifts, abilities, feelings, and an intelligence we might not be aware of because we, as a species, made a move some centuries ago to put our trust in science rather than the spiritual side of our existence. I am not trying to demean or minimize the importance of science, but I am certainly putting emphasis on my belief in balance of thought. Sometimes things just are as they are and do not need to be explained. Maybe people should learn to let things be what they are supposed to be without always feeling the need to seek answers or explanations.

I can't remember the year, but Kate was located in a pasture behind our house with three other horses. She was being quite bossy, but then again, she did that wherever she went. Matt would get his lawn chair and walk towards the fence carrying his children's Bible with him, along with a glass of sweet tea. The Bible was a gift at birth from his godparents. Kate would see him coming, and knowing the routine, she would walk to the fence and hang her head as he read Bible stories to her.

Matt reading his Bible to Kate

No other horse would intrude on them. It was her time with her master. The other horses knew Kate and knew better than to get nosy. This was not a normal occurrence in the horse world. Normally, when a horse comes to the fence and a human is around, the others will want to know why and they will come too. It didn't matter how long Matt read; Kate would hang her head, relax, get that far-away look in her eye, and listen to the cadence of his voice. This happened on a regular basis, and she never failed to join Matt and listen, never tiring of the stories. After all these years, I am very thankful that I not only have the picture in my mind but I have one to show you. Thanks for the memories, Katie.

≈

Early in Kate's seventh year with us, I noticed some things about her that troubled me. Sometimes she would stumble where she was normally a sure-footed little mare. Other times, when she was sleeping or deeply relaxing, she would fall to her knees. Horses normally sleep standing up with three legs locked in position and one rear leg cocked upward but still touching the ground. It is not normal for a horse to fall; it just doesn't happen. So I began to watch her more closely.

When you think something is wrong with a horse, you look for classic signs, and Katie did not exhibit any of them. She wasn't in apparent distress; her respirations, breathing, and temperature were normal. Her appetite and water consumption were normal. Her bowels and urine were normal. In other words, she appeared to be doing just fine, except for the fact that she sometimes fell down when sleeping.

I have had a great working relationship with veterinarians both in my home area and the area around Lexington. So I started making phone calls inquiring about the possibility of horses being diagnosed with narcolepsy. To my surprise I found out horses could have a diagnosis of narcolepsy just like humans. No one I talked to was convinced Kate had it because her problem only happened when she was already sleeping and never (that I witnessed) at other times. They described narcolepsy symptoms as being wide awake one second and a split second later being fast asleep. This description did not fit what was happening to Kate. Given that she was apparently healthy otherwise, we decided to watch her closely. There was little they could do even if she did have narcolepsy other than give her an official diagnosis.

We went through spells during that year when things would seem normal and other times where we would see her stumble or fall a couple of times a day while sleeping. All her other signs were normal. Then one day we were eating dinner with the doors and windows open when we heard a very loud crash from outside. We thought there had been an accident, but as we looked outside, we couldn't see anything amiss. There was no apparent accident, and all the horses were accounted for and grazing. It was another one of those unexplainable occurrences that sometime happens, but then again, maybe not.

About three weeks later, it happened once again, and again we went outside to see what had made the noise. Everything looked normal except for Kate. She was barely able to hold her head up and was acting real wobbly. I went out into the field to check on her, and it was quite apparent that she could not see me. She had a small cut on her head, and from the way she was acting, she couldn't see a thing. She wouldn't blink when I put my finger on her eye and could not seem to focus on anything. Further investigation revealed a big dent in the side of the run-in shed where she had shelter from the weather and sun. She had apparently gone blind, panicked, and run into the shed at full speed. It is a wonder she didn't break her neck. I made a quick call to the vet and put her in a stall.

By the time the vet arrived, Katie was once again acting like her old self. She did not show any signs of blindness. We talked about all the symptoms she had been exhibiting and nothing made sense. He thought she may have been spooked by something (like a snake) and darted into the side of the shed, knocking herself loopy. It was possible, and I wish that was what happened, but I was pretty sure there must be another explanation. After making sure she could see, I put her back out and into a pasture by herself. Two days later, it happened again.

Unfortunately, this would be the last time. I once again called the veterinarian, and he came for another examination. Before he arrived, Kate had a seizure and trembled violently for a short period of time. While the vet was checking her, she had another. She wasn't blind, but something neurological was going on in the poor girl's brain. Given her advancing age, the advice was to put her to sleep. I paid the vet, thanked him, and told him I would let him know what I decided later.

Then I started making phone calls as I searched for hope. I consulted with every animal doctor I knew and was told the same thing by all. It was time, and we had to consider Kate might hurt herself again or hurt someone else while having a seizure. Something was going on that could not be fixed.

I realized then it was time for me to man up. I had to deliver the news to the two other people who loved this little hard-headed mare deeply that it was time to let Kate go. The tears flowed freely from everyone. I think this is one of the hardest jobs a parent has to do, but it is a job that can't be avoided if parents encourage their children to include animals in the family. If you have pets, you will deliver this news eventually. Our yard is dotted with the graves of beloved pets like dogs, cats, and turtles. Words have been spoken over all of them, and the words have always been heartfelt. This time it was more difficult for me. This was my son's first horse, and he had grown up with her. As a family, we were devastated and heartbroken.

≈

The time was set for the vet to attend to Kate's final needs. Decisions had been made and the tears dried, although it seems to me that the tears dry on your face but continue to flow in your heart for years, if not forever. The emotional attachments resulting from investment in our relationships with animals, especially horses, are profound. This part of the ritual was up to me. I was the one to lead her for the last time. I decided to lead her between the barns and groom her one last time. Kate loved the attention and the rhythmic stroke of the brush on her soft coat. She was attentive to the words I spoke and had a far-away look in her eyes that I had seen so often while she was being read to. I know she felt loved, safe, and at home.

Chad Bailey (the vet) had arrived while I was talking to her and waited for me to finish before preparing the injections. I said my good-byes full of the absolute belief that death is never the end but a transition for all living things. My faith did not prevent me from burning with hurt, not only for my wife and son but also for myself. I would and still do miss that pretty little mare. I appreciated the gifts of smiles, laughter, love, and even the exasperation that at times she gifted me with over the years we shared together. I will always cherish the memories.

Chad administered the shots, and shortly afterward Kate was peacefully gone. Chad is a wonderful vet and always sheds a tear when he has to put an animal down. That day was no different. I appreciate him for his big heart and caring treatment of all animals. After he left I sat with Kate for a long time, talking and laughing over some of the antics I had seen her pull over the years. I cut off a piece of her mane and tail and took them with me as I returned to the house. Then I wrote a poem. I am not a poet, and it may sound juvenile, but the words came from somewhere deep inside me.

Old Kate
January 13, 2005

Black, brown, and white,
A tri-colored mare,
Such a beauty when younger
Made most cowboys stare.

A Father's Day gift,
Strange as it seems,
To a boy barely six
Wearing little man jeans

'Twas a lesson to be
Learned it was thought
By the man called Dad
That for you I was bought.

The lesson was learned
By you very well:
Care for her kindly
And with pride you will swell.

You read me the Bible,
Combed my coat, mane, and tail.
You showed me your love
Every day without fail.

You cared for my knees
With medicines and lotions.
And worried about me
As you saw my slowed motions.

You grew up that day
The decision was made
To let me go quietly.
My memory won't fade.

So here's a piece of my tail
To remember me by
On those days when I gallop
Through your mind's eye.

And a piece of my mane,
Windblown with braiding,
As a reminder of where we have been
And a promise that with
God I'll be waiting.

Richard D. Rowland (Dad)
For Matt
January 21, 2005

Like I said, it came from the heart. I braided the mane and the tail separately, and to this day, they reside in our house. Kate's memory is as fresh today as it was over eight years ago. And Kate, I finally told your story, dear. See you someday.

Part Two

COMING CLEAN AND FACING FEAR

*There are only two ways to live your life. One
is as though nothing is a miracle. The other
is as though everything is a miracle.*
—Albert Einstein

Full moon on a cloudy night courtesy Richard D. Rowland

Chapter One

Mind-Numbing News

I HAVE NO DOUBT YOU have wondered what could have happened in my life to change the black-and-white, right-or-wrong, hardheaded, curmudgeonly person you knew and tolerated into the person I am today. A person who evolved into one who sees the world we exist in to be full of varying shades of gray. A person who has become a believer in the overwhelming proof of a magical energy that surrounds us and one who is convinced that coincidence does not exist. I have become a man who is certain that he has faced his own mortality head on and walked away a believer that we are immortal. The words often attributed to C.S. Lewis, "You don't have a soul. You are a soul. You have a body," has become a mantra of sorts. The explanation will be a condensed version of the past five years of my life. Please accompany me on a short side trip through my mind and find out how I arrived at a place of peace, contentment, and gratitude for all that I have been blessed to discover.

I guess this would be a good time to issue an apology to my friends and my extended family for not previously being honest and forthcoming about my health and hardiness. I did not keep you in the dark or maintain secrecy because I did not want to share with you or because we were not close enough for me to confide in you. I beg you to understand that this was and is my journey to travel, and I had to find my own way, just as there may come a time in your life when you will have to search within to find meaning. In my case, I searched through a vast amount of information in order to set a course for the eventual arrival at my nirvana. Along the way, I did have the support of my immediate family and the few medical professionals whom I trust. Now I am here, I am home.

My journey began on Thursday, August 21, 2008, with these words: "You have cancer. It is a blood cancer called multiple myeloma. It is relatively rare, and it is incurable. No matter what we do for you, you have three to five years to live at the most, and many people do not live that long." My long-time family doctor spoke these words to my wife and me during an appointment to discuss the results of some blood tests that had been performed earlier that month. I should have known that the news was not going to be good when they asked for Jennifer to be with me for the appointment, but cancer never entered my mind as a possibility. Cancer happened to other people, not to me, or so I thought.

It is hard to explain the weight these words carried when suddenly placed directly upon my shoulders. Up until this point in my life, death was not something I gave much thought to. Sure, knowledge of death's existence was stored somewhere far in the cloud covered back of my mind but it was rarely given any attention. Like most of you I was too busy living life to think about my own mortality. As a matter of fact, prior to hearing these words, I still felt I was immortal and the magic proving this feeling to be true would be apparent long before I could die. The words carried a shock through my core that seemed to reverberate without end. I trembled on the inside but maintained a questioning outward appearance. The words carrying this perceived death sentence were delivered by someone I trusted, believed in, and truly thought was a friend. I had always believed he had me and my family's health and longevity at heart, and I also believed he was a conservative doctor regarding medications. I revisited these and other beliefs during the next five years and came to different conclusions. I should go on to say that the effect of his words sucked any idea of healing from me as quickly as if a hole were opened in my soul that rapidly allowed every expectation of an optimistic outcome to pour out, robbing me of the very thing you must have in order to heal or maintain life, and that is *hope.*

Little did I know that I had many lessons being sent my way that would contain explicit directions about how to repair the hole and restore my missing hope. After privately drying the tears of fear and disappointment, my wife and I left the doctor's office and set off on the first steps of the rest of our journey together. As we walked past another examination room, we heard the same doctor laughing loudly with another patient, who we assumed was fortunate enough to not be receiving a death sentence that day. I will say that I do not envy doctors. It must take a terrific toll on them emotionally to have to shift their feelings from one minute to the next, bringing hope to those they see as curable and delivering news like mine to others, all the while believing wholly in science and no other power to help those in need. I guess that may sound a little angry, but trust me, you haven't seen the levels my anger could reach yet.

The ride home was thankfully short and understandably quiet as we held hands. Both of us had many emotions that needed to be sorted out. One thing I was adamant about was that I did not want anyone to know, including my then fifteen-year-old son. Young people in that age group have enough stresses on their shoulders without trying to carry the weight of a parent's possible passing as well. In hindsight, maybe this wasn't a good idea, but it was what I wanted at the time.

Believe it or not, I saw myself as weak and did not want anyone else to view me in that manner. I was a retired sergeant from the Kentucky State Police and prior to that had spent two tours in Vietnam. I was hardened and honed by life, and I did not want to be viewed as sick and fragile. In some ways I still don't want that, which makes this surge of honesty difficult. I didn't and still do not want any pity parties on my behalf.

One thing Jennifer and I did agree on was the need for a second opinion. During the down time between opinions, I made a decision to personally take charge of my health. I told my wife that I was going to stop taking the prescription medicines I was currently taking on a regular basis, which totaled five that time. All of them were, I believed, conservatively prescribed, but I felt they were no longer helping and may have been doing more harm than good.

Seven years prior to this bump in my road, I was a healthy, exercising, hardworking man with little in the way of medical problems. I was retired, but I worked hard on the family horse farm daily. Then I went to my trusted family doctor for a nagging back issue. While there, he ordered and performed a non-fasting blood test for cholesterol levels. True blood tests of this nature are normally performed after fasting overnight in order to get a more reliable result. A week later he called me and told me I had to start taking a prescription medicine to control elevated blood cholesterol. I asked what the numbers were and he said, "185 for the total and the rest were in line."

I said, "Doc, they have always been in that range."

The doctor said "I know, but the rules have changed, and with your family history, we need to get your levels in the 165 range or lower."

My father had died of a heart attack at the age of sixty-three. Keep in mind that my father was a Purple Heart recipient and a combat veteran of World War II. He ate a diet filled with saturated fats and had other habits detrimental to his health and longevity that I did not share. But, being a dutiful man who put doctors on a pedestal, I agreed to take the prescription as ordered, believing I was doing something positive for my health.

Within the first week to ten days of beginning the medication, I started having very intense pain and leg cramps. Calls to the doctor and blood tests indicated the pills were not the problem, but he changed to another cholesterol medicine anyway. Six different brands of cholesterol medicine later, I was told the pills were not causing the problem, my blood levels were perfect, and I would live a long time if I kept taking the medication as prescribed.

I believed what I was told and continued taking the pills, but the problems continued to mount up. I started having heartburn all the time and asked my doctor if the cholesterol pills might be the cause. I was told they were not, and I was given a prescription for a proton pump inhibitor (PPI). The stomach problems continued even with the PPI, and I had two ulcers in a six-month period. Within the first year, I had to have my gallbladder removed, which was coated with cholesterol crystals. I kept inquiring about the relation of the medicine to the problems I was having, and my trusted physician kept reassuring me that the medicine was not causing the problem.

The leg pain and digestive problems continued. In another attempt to control the leg pain, I was given a prescription for a medicine given to diabetics for neuropathy. Once again, I returned to the doctor, and this time I broke down and cried in his office because of the pain. All of a sudden, depression was the problem, and I was put on an antidepressant.

Is anyone noticing my inability to draw arrows from my problems to the prescription medicines? I was a hell of a police officer, don't you think? I didn't see the glowing neon directional arrows because I believed in Western medicine. I believed in my doctor. Things really came to a head when I found myself with yet another prescription meant to counter side effects from the other medicines I was taking. I felt like my life was spiraling out of control. I was losing weight, I didn't have any energy, and I couldn't sleep. Suddenly, food didn't have flavor anymore, and even though my wife is a wonderfully talented cook, I found myself eating only out of habit.

The final straw came just prior to the multiple myeloma diagnosis when I was diagnosed with Barrett's esophagus, a precancerous condition of the esophagus with dysphasia or cellular changes indicating an imminent possibility of cancer. I was told it was incurable, that it would change into cancer eventually, and the treatment was four PPI's a day. I reminded the specialist I was seeing for the issue that I was already taking one PPI a day to no avail, but they were steadfast in their treatment plan. After less than one week on their plan, I was too weak to walk to the barns without resting halfway there.

The die was cast, and the decision was made by me and seconded by my wife to stop the madness. We properly disposed of all my prescription medicine, and I stopped cold turkey. I knew that stopping that way would not be medically advisable, but at that point in my life, I was no longer sure I trusted my health to Western medicine advice.

Ten days later, we were still awaiting a second opinion. We had gone to Nashville for a horse-related show, trying to live life as usual. However, the undercurrent of sadness and finality had become stronger and overwhelmed our attempts at normalcy.

I remember distinctly awakening on a Saturday morning and telling my wife, "Jennifer, I am hungry."

Jennifer said, "Hang on a few more minutes, I'm almost ready, and we will head down for breakfast."

I said, "You don't understand. I haven't been hungry in over two years, but *I am hungry!*" I was famished and have pretty much stayed that way since I got the prescription drugs out of my system.

After a few phone calls to some doctor friends, we decided to go to the Veterans Affairs Hospital. Multiple myeloma is a cancer related to exposure to the herbicide dioxin, better known as Agent Orange. I was in Vietnam, so I was viewed as having been exposed to the chemical. Appointments were made and kept, tests were performed and performed again, and finally I had an appointment to talk to another doctor. The date was September 16, 2008, and this doctor delivered the same death sentence but with a little flair. She spent most of the appointment looking at her watch, the clock, never making eye contact, and playing with her hair. She told me that without treatment, I would be very sick by November, which was three months from then. Maybe I was her first death sentence delivery, and she was nervous—who knows? I do know she needed to work on her delivery.

After she exited the room, Jennifer and I also left, not bothering to wait for her to return with printed information. This doctor had given me a gift I sorely needed, and that was the gift of anger. I became mad at anyone in the medical community who would not offer hope. I became mad at doctors who pretend they have the insight or their personal crystal ball to judge how long or well you will live. Plainly put, I went from an emotional state of despair to being absolutely livid. After stopping the medicine, my rapid improvement gave me a much-needed glimpse of life the way it used to be, and I wanted desperately to get back there. So instead of doing as we were told, we took a right turn and began to travel a different path. The motivation I felt inside came from the anger, but it led to a place called peace, which was exactly where I needed to be in order to grow into the new me.

Chapter Two

An Awakening

S igmund Freud once said, "When we attempt to imagine death, we perceive ourselves as spectators." I do believe he is spot-on in his estimation of this issue, because that is what happened to me when thinking about my own possible demise. My mind seemed to be outside, looking at my body as if it were something foreign. I would also find myself believing what many others in his field had to say about death and dying, especially Elizabeth Kubler-Ross, whom I found to be extremely enlightening. She wrote, "Fear and guilt are the enemies of man." I learned that these are very powerful negative motivators.

I should also let you know that on more than one occasion early in the process of acceptance, I wailed and cried to God, or the Creator, or one of the many other monikers used to name the Deity most of us envision. I cussed him. I why'd him. I begged him. I wanted to know why this happened to me when I have so much left to do. How dare he stand by and let this happen to me! Had anyone within earshot heard these arguments and been unaware of the situation, they would have thought me daft at the least. But it was not long after these "talks" that I began to witness many strange and wonderful things, and those things brought sunshine to replace the darkness that had limited my view of the road on which I was walking. The things I experienced during this learning phase carried the gift of hope and guidance that would lead me onward.

When you receive a diagnosis like the one I did, you never forget dates and what day of the week things happened on. Dates and days become anniversaries etched forever in your memory. I received my diagnosis on a Thursday. That particular year, we were very involved in the local farmers' market and sold organic vegetables, herbs, breads, and homemade soap on Tuesdays, Thursdays, and Saturdays of each week. We had missed the Thursday sale because of my appointment and decided that regardless of our mental state we would go Saturday, hoping the social time would put our troubles on the back burner for a few hours.

Bright and early on August 23, 2008, we arrived at the farmer's market and set up our wares. Around 9:30 a.m., an elderly lady walked under our canopy and asked if we would mind if she got out of the sun and rested for a minute. I got up and offered her my chair, and she sat down. The first words she uttered after sitting down are imprinted on my memory and resonate there to this day. She said, "Don't listen to doctors or believe in everything they say. They can be wrong." She had my total attention from that moment forward. She did not know my situation or me, so just exactly how she could state something that hit so close to my center was quite astonishing. Even though I discovered much later that I knew her daughter, I had never met this lady before. I became enthralled by her stories and gave her my full attention.

As it turns out, she was a widow, originally from England. She had married a young American solder at the end of World War II and moved to the United States. They were living in Texas when he died many years later, after a long and happy marriage. She went on to tell us that she sold out and moved here to Kentucky to live with her daughter because she was told she would be losing her eyesight very soon. When she arrived here, she found out that she had been misdiagnosed, and instead of the disease she was told she had, she simply needed cataract surgery. She now sees just fine. Her visit and message were not only timely but also somewhat prophetic. I felt as if she were a messenger sent to ease my worries and to tell me to chart my future with open eyes. I listened eagerly to her message.

Many things happened in rapid succession after Jennifer and I started this journey together. I must tell you that my wife is a holistic nutritionist by training, and I have always referred to her as my little hippie chick or my island girl. She is one of the most spiritual people I know and has always been very open minded. I, on the other hand, would previously have pooh-poohed the spiritual side of things and believed strictly in science and facts. Notice I said previously. When Western medicine offered little or no hope, I found myself searching for answers and desperately seeking a healthy dose of optimism concerning my longevity.

At Jennifer's direction, the first thing we did was search for a doctor of naturopathy, and we were lucky enough to find one locally. This was my first experience with one of the many other sides of medicine. The doctor was also someone I had known for years without knowing his beliefs. Although I walked out of that first visit with many supplements, the most important thing I walked out with was hope. He described disease as a result of excesses in the body. A lifetime of putting the wrong things in your system is like a water glass filling and overflowing. When the body can no longer handle the impurities and harmful chemicals we subject it to through a bad diet and terrible habits, disease is the result. Although the comparison may at first seem simplistic, that was exactly the way I needed to hear it instead of being fed big words and scientific data.

Naturalists do not believe in taking cholesterol medication to lower a person's levels to an unreasonably low number. They see inflammation as the cause of heart disease and don't blame the cholesterol that your body needs to function properly. Also, they do not believe in the use of a PPI. Their school of thought is that as you age, your body does not always produce *enough* acid. As a result, food stays inside your stomach too long, causing heartburn and esophageal erosion. Therefore, they want you to take acid with a meal to insure that food moves through the digestion process faster. I find it amazing how different these two factions are when it comes to disease management. This natural doctor explained that Western medicine is probably the best in the world at putting out the fires like traumas, heart attacks, and strokes, to mention a few, but it isn't the best at building the body back to health. They make really good firemen but might not be the best construction workers if, as is often the case, they only treat the symptoms and not the cause.

As I look back now, after becoming much more informed, I understand and embrace the naturalist view. I have met many Western medicine doctors who may agree with some of the beliefs of the naturalist, but Western medicine is ruled by the American Medical Association (AMA). If doctors want to keep their license to practice, they have to abide by the AMA guidelines. It is here that I am reminded of a Chinese proverb my naturalist friend uses often: "The frog at the bottom of the well fails to grasp the vastness of the sky." I believe that in the process of being ruled by the AMA, doctors don't get to see all of the possibilities that exist, nor are they able to take advantage of other modalities that can affect healing.

Next, I was introduced to another practitioner of the healing arts. This one was a registered nurse who used to work not only at a hospital but also at a hospice center. Now she runs her own office and practices/ teaches Reiki and Jin Shin Jyutsu. She makes sure you understand she is not acting as a doctor or nurse. One of her specialties uses energy from without, and the other uses energy from within your body to assist in healing. The ancient belief is energy travels through channels inside the body, and blockage of the energy results in disease or discomfort. Opening these blockages enables the body to heal. This is just a simple and brief explanation, but I believe it gives you the idea.

It was during my first appointment with her that I had an absolutely amazing, life-changing event occur. As someone who had retired from law enforcement, proof still stood all alone atop my list of the necessary requirements for me to believe in something. After this first session, I became a believer, and the need for absolute proof went out the window as a prerequisite for assurance of truth. Instead belief, as well as faith, jumped to the top of the list.

During my first treatment session with her, she had me lie on a table in a darkened room, fully clothed. There was music playing lightly in the background, and I was told to close my eyes, give a prayer of intention to the Creator for what I hoped would occur, and relax. Those were the only requirements. My prayer was for peace about my convictions concerning the direction we had decided I would travel. I wanted a sign of some kind to let me know everything would be all right. I found it easy to relax because Native American flute music was playing and I am a fan of the genre. The session lasted about forty-five minutes. My wife was in the waiting room and would soon become a witness to something special.

About twenty minutes into the session, a terrible storm began. There was lightning, thunder rattling the walls, and you could hear sheets of rain hitting the building. I was mesmerized by the cacophony of the summer thunderstorm. I also mentally drifted a little, because we were in an extreme period of dryness and the thought entered my mind that we sure did need the rain for our pasture. The storm lasted about fifteen to twenty minutes, and shortly afterwards my session was complete. Jan (the practitioner) quietly said, "Lie there and relax. I'll be right back. I have to go close the windows on my car because I had them down during the storm." She returned two or three minutes later, and I asked her if her car got soaked during the rainstorm. She said, "It didn't rain on my car, and the parking lot is dry."

My wife and I walked out of the office with Jan and made the trip all the way around the outside of the medical office building. Not a drop of rain had fallen on any car in the parking lot—not one! The lot was as dry as it had been when we went inside. However, if you took a few steps back and looked on the roof, the air conditioning units on the roof were wet, as well as anything else that rose in height above the roofline. Everything on the roof was wet! Off in the distance we could see a small raincloud moving east.

It had apparently only rained on the building I was in and nowhere else. We all agreed that we heard the storm; we heard the rain hitting the building and could feel and smell the energy a summer storm leaves in the air. I left there knowing I had received my sign and the path I was on was a correct one. Other things would happen to me during future sessions. One time, I felt as if I were being pushed down into the bed. I tried to raise my arms but couldn't. Other times, as I meditated, I would see three-dimensional flashes of people and objects. Suddenly, doors were being opened, and I was walking through with an open mind, searching for more enlightenment and growth.

I went to Jan for over three years, once or twice a week. She taught me a self-help regime which I still practice every day of my life. My wife and I both went to Reiki classes and became level two Reiki practitioners. My belief in energy from both within and without is strong.

Throughout this early period of awakening, I was witness to several other occurrences that made me take time to question my previous assumptions about life and all the wonder surrounding it. We used to have to drag or carry a water hose about five hundred feet to a frost-proof hydrant in order to fill water troughs for two of the pastures. During a trip to water the horses one hot day, I was standing in the blazing sun when a bee landed on my chest. Normally, I would have swatted the bee, killed it, and been thankful I hadn't been stung. Today however, armed with my growing appreciation for all things living, I left it alone. I not only left it alone, I started petting his wings. I haven't a clue what made me do such a thing. I would lightly stroke the wings, one at a time, from front to back. I did this the whole time I was filling one trough. I thought when I moved to the other trough, the bee would probably leave, but it did not. I kept petting his wings even while walking about.

The bee stayed with me as I filled two water troughs and carried the hose five hundred feet back to the house. This entire experience brought me an intense feeling of peace and love for the world and all within it. The bee left my chest when the chore was complete, and I headed into the house. I went in much richer than I was when I left. In a later conversation with a nurse practitioner that we came to know, I discovered that bees are religious symbols. I told her this story just as I have related it to you. She said that bees are etched in a chain-like fashion around the top of some stone columns in Rome and that bees are a symbol of miracles, because aerodynamically bumble bees are not supposed to be able to fly due to their body size and lack of large wings. The mention of miracles brought me a further message of hope which I welcomed.

If you are travelling a path similar to mine and dealing with a disease of some sort, I want to make sure you know that bouts of absolute depression are cyclic and will occur more frequently early on as you come to terms with the changes in your life. I was having one of those emotionally down days on a beautiful summer day. My best friend Lee and my wife Jennifer had joined me on the deck to talk and enjoy the weather. Also in attendance was Sarge, our golden retriever.

As we were discussing things no one really wanted to talk about, we received a visitor. Out of the corner of my eye, I noticed a bird slowing its descent in order to land on the roof of the house. That in itself was not odd and actually happened often, but the type of bird was very unusual. It was a pigeon—not an ordinary pigeon, but a beautiful pigeon with a solid golden hue like none I had ever seen before. I had seen pigeons in town before and around interstate bridges, but I had never seen a pigeon around the farm.

The pigeon landed on the edge of the roof directly in front of me. Its focus was entirely on me and stayed that way as if no one else was there, not even the dog. It would walk to and fro on the roof edge but was never out of eye contact with me. Its eyes drew me to it, and it was as if it were looking directly into my soul. If the pigeon's color were not amazing enough, its eyes were ringed in gold as well. I had never viewed such a beautiful bird, nor have I seen one since that day. It stayed for forty-five minutes to an hour. All of us stared and talked about the bird with wonder, curious about where it could have possibly come from and why it was so openly interested in me.

At one point I scooped some wild bird seed from a feed can and placed it on the deck rail directly beside me. To my astonishment, the bird flew down and ate not three feet from me, still keeping its attention in my direction. It did not pay any attention to Sarge, who was very interested in the bird. My friend Lee held Sarge's collar and petted him to keep him calm. After eating, the pigeon flew back up onto the roof and went back to gazing at me.

Although I felt like I could have stayed there with the bird for hours, it was time for supper, and I was ready to eat. As we rose to go into the house, the bird looked at me intensely one more time and flew to the barn. The barn is about one hundred feet from the house, and there is an electric service pole in front of it. The pigeon landed on top of the pole and remained there looking toward the house for two more hours before flying off or simply disappearing. In other words, it was there one moment and gone the next, never to be seen again.

Many people I have shared this story with have told me that they have been taught that God can send messengers in the form of animals, and I now believe this to be true. Many of the books I have read since my new life started contain similar stories about animals bringing peace to the people who need it most. The pigeon was here for a reason, and I am convinced the reason was to bring stillness and wonder to me in order to silence my mind.

Shortly after the golden-hued pigeon arrived, my focus moved away from my problem and was directed to that beautiful creature. I felt peace, wonder, contentment, gratitude, and many more breathtaking emotions in its presence. I had completely forgotten how utterly depressed I was prior to its arrival in my life. Was it a gift? I am sure of it. The magic of the blessing lifted me out of the hole I had created for myself, and I felt full of hope once again.

There are times since that day when the now very infrequent bouts of depression try to take over my mood that I remember the bird and the gift of peace it granted me on a beautiful summer day. Its gift continues to work magic to this day. The universe is a wondrous place filled with moments resembling this one. I think before my eyes were opened to things like this, I might have thought something was wrong with the bird and there was probably a scientific reason for its presence. Now I know differently. Coincidence doesn't exist. Things happen as they are supposed to. Our souls are immortal and wonder abounds. Just open your eyes and mind to the possibilities and receive them.

I could go on writing about many more personal experiences I have witnessed, wonders such as the three I have just relayed to you, but let me leave you with this: open your mind to positive possibilities and view things that happen to you in a light separate from science. Believe in the unbelievable. Look at the world through the eyes you possessed as a child, through a mind untainted by scientific reason and the planted perceptions you have been carrying since you lost your youthful wonder and a mature rationale became the norm. Please do not let hope die or be stolen from you by well-intended people who may believe they have all the answers. I am convinced they do not know all there is to know.

Chapter Three

The Proof Is in the Evidence

NEALE DONALD WALSCH SAID, "FEAR is an acronym in the English language for False Evidence Appearing Real." I have mentioned my law enforcement background a few times in this book, so it should come as no surprise to you that I would search for any evidence which might exist to help ease my mind. I needed to quiet any lingering doubt. My initial quest began around the same time I was witnessing the magical things I related in the previous chapter. I found myself wanting answers to life's oldest questions. Is this all there is? What am I here for? Is there some form of life after death? Where do other people diagnosed with cancer find peace? How will my family go on without me? So many questions begged for my attention, but no concrete or simple answers seemed to be obvious.

So I started down another path in my search for answers, and the answers came from reading many books, articles, and data from support groups. I loved and appreciated all of the information I received because it was filled with hope and documented miracles. When you are hoping for a miracle, read about people who have received one; don't read the mortality report for the particular disease with which you have been diagnosed. If miracles can happen for one person, find out how they can happen for you and everyone else. While I am at it, do not give any energy to the disease you have been diagnosed with by saying you have it. I have never said, "I have _____," and I never will. I feel that would give more power to the disease. I want the power to stay within me and be used in a positive manner.

Books rapidly became a major source of inspiration for me—not the only source, but a major one. You will probably also need several inspirational sources if you someday find yourself facing the same challenges I was confronting. I do not want to offend anyone with my beliefs. I know there will be critics of my beliefs and this book. I do not want to step on the toes of organized religion, and I do not want to lead you or negatively affect or feed your beliefs. I just want to let you know how I found peace amid despair. Whether you follow my path or not is your choice to make. What is important here is you find a path to follow that *you* believe in and can pursue with all the energy you have.

I keep a journal where I write about the events of each day and the gratitude I have at some point felt during that day. At the end of every journal entry, I write the words "I am healed" and "I believe" in capital letters. I firmly believe both of those statements. As a matter of fact, I think the words *I am*, when followed by positive phrases, are possibly the two most powerful words you can use to heal your mind, body, and spirit. But remember, they are just as powerful if followed by those negatives that you really don't want but just happen to fear and vocalize. My message to you is to find your own path, stay the course with a strong faith in your beliefs, and discover peace and hope in your daily life.

I would like to share with you insights and messages I received from some of the authors who have helped me in my journey. Almost to a person, these are well-educated and well-respected people. They are not quacks or charlatans who had a dream one night or an idea and wrote a book only with the idea of making money. They are researchers, visionaries, and trusted members of their communities.

Several years before I received the diagnosis I now live with, my wife tried to get me to read a book entitled *Many Lives, Many Masters* by Brian L.Weiss, M.D. I never would read it. I guess it wasn't the proper time for me, and I had no desire to read what I considered at that time to be nonsense. When she tried again in 2008, I listened. Reading this book started the exploration which eventually changed my belief system completely. It satisfied the need in me for proof in order to believe something has merit.

Dr. Weiss is a highly respected psychiatrist. He was educated at Columbia University and Yale Medical School. He is also Chairman Emeritus of Psychiatry at the Mount Sinai Medical Center in Miami. In my mind, this satisfied the scientific pedigree I currently needed evidence of in order to believe.

Dr. Weiss is a traditionally trained medical doctor with a specialty in psychiatry. He originally believed, as most other doctors believe, in medicine based upon science, research, chemical balances, and therapy, among other things. Through his practice, he became a believer in reincarnation. *Many Lives, Many Masters* is the story of how his beliefs changed through his patients and the fact that they knew things they shouldn't know. Their experiences could not be explained through scientific Western medicine. He was able to validate their experiences through research into the past.

His research led me on my own quest for others who have delved into this subject, and there are many. Several of these authors documented cases of reincarnation, including very young children being able to speak in a foreign language and know people from countries other than the country of their birth.

The outcome of reading these books was a deep and abiding belief that we have been here before and will be here again. These books explained some of the experiences I had as a child with the phenomenon of déjà vu, which according to Wikipedia, means "having a strong sensation that an event or experience currently being experienced has been experienced in the past." I had these sensations a lot as a child, but they faded as I aged. Almost to a researcher/author, this was explained by saying that when we are young and closer to the time when we returned, our memories are stronger. As we age, the memories and feelings weaken and fade away. I finished reading this series of books with a sense of calm and a hope for what awaits all of us. There will be a journey home eventually; the question that plagues us is the issue of timing.

One of the next of the many books I read was *Conversations with God: An Uncommon Dialogue* by Neale Donald Walsch. Although there will be some who take issue with the book, I found it to be refreshing at the least and at the most insightful and inspiring. I always had trouble understanding how a loving God could seemingly become revengeful and figuratively spank you for taking advantage of the gift of free will that had been bestowed upon you. This was just one of the numerous issues that I had difficulty understanding, and the book explained many of them to my satisfaction. I found my mind was being challenged to think in new ways, and I was up for the challenge.

Although I am basically mentioning books that inspired the change in me chronologically, I would have to say I believe the book *Love, Medicine and Miracles* by Bernie S. Siegel, MD, would otherwise be at the top of the list. Dr. Siegel went to Colgate College, is a graduate of Cornell University of Medicine, and received his training as a surgeon at Yale New Haven Hospital, among others. He is also a doctor who believes in and has witnessed miracles unexplainable in modern medicine, and, I might add, his willingness to talk and write about them might be contrary to AMA guidelines. Through his writings, beliefs, and research, he tells of cancer patients getting well and about others who weren't cured but lived a better quality of life. I feel all of his books are a must-read for anyone living with a life-ending diagnosis. His message is one of hope and love, and it fed the roots of the fledging sapling of optimism starting to grow in my soul, helping it to become strong yet flexible, like an oak. I was starting to change, and I liked what I felt. Thank you, Dr. Siegel, for your message.

I would like to share this quote from the back page of Dr. Siegel's book, *Love, Medicine and Miracles.*

Unconditional love is the most powerful stimulant of the immune system. The truth is: love heals. Miracles happen to exceptional patients every day—patients who have the courage to love, those who have the courage to work with their doctors to participate in and influence their own recovery.

You may think it odd I chose a quote from the back cover of a book that contains so many inspirational quotes, but in this case that fact is important. I picked out this book by myself; it had not been recommended to me previously. A strong, intuitive sense led me to pick it up, even though I had never heard of Dr. Siegel prior to that day. Reading his quote on the back cover led me to read not only this book but every book published by Dr. Siegel. If you need to hear a message of hope, please read Dr. Siegel's books. I wrote to Dr. Siegel recently and told him about my diagnosis and the endeavor with this book and thanked him for the message of hope I had received in 2008 through his books. His reply was, "Richard, my compliment is you are not normal but far better than normal. Peace, Bernie." His motivational words continue to bring me just that—peace.

Then, as I continued along the path of searching and learning, I found a book titled *What Does That Mean? Exploring Mind, Meaning, and Mysteries,* by Eldon Taylor. This was one of those books that once I started reading it, I couldn't put it down. It was not only a page turner but one I have reread many times since and learned something fresh with each new visit that helped me with the healing process. I developed an affinity for the writings of Eldon Taylor not only because of his message of hope and a continued existence after death, but also because we had experienced a mirror-like existence on life's journey. Mr. Taylor has a background in law enforcement, just like me. He has been heavily involved in horses throughout his life, including time running a horse stabling business, as have I. Even more curious, he had the joy of witnessing a situation much like the one I experienced and documented in the story that started this book, *And They All Said Goodbye.* It was quite wonderful to find I was not the only person to witness such an event and write about it. It was as if an objective observer validated my experience.

Towards the end of Mr. Taylor's book, he writes,

> This book has been all about the stuff that's most dear to our hearts. Who are we? What is life and what does it mean? Is there a purpose? Is there a God? Are we the product of some cosmic joke or accident? How do we answer these questions and the host of others that arise when we seriously look at the meaning of life?

Mr. Taylor does a superb job of answering those questions and many more throughout this book. Are you looking for hope? If you are, this is the kind of book you need to be reading.

One book I found extremely enlightening and encouraging was *Proof of Heaven: A Neurosurgeon's Journey into the Afterlife* by Eben Alexander, MD. Dr. Alexander is a well-known neurosurgeon who personally experienced a NDE (near-death experience) after a bout of bacterial meningitis left him in an extended coma without any brain function. I will not give away an amazing surprise contained within the story, but I can assure you, you will be astonished by Dr. Alexander's accounting of a continued existence after our bodies cease to exist. Keep in mind that this book was written by a medical doctor who specializes in brain function. It has been his life's study. He ends up becoming a convinced believer in a continued life after death because of his experience, whereas before his beliefs were science based. I consider this book a must read for anyone going through end-of-life challenges.

The next piece of evidence, as I call it, is a book by Pim van Lommel, MD, titled *Consciousness Beyond Life: The Science of the Near-Death Experience*. Dr. van Lommel is a cardiologist who practiced at the Rijnstate Hospital in the Netherlands. He was published in the prestigious medical journal *The Lancet* on the subjects of near-death experiences and consciousness. Dr. Lommel completed a twenty-five-year study on the subject of NDEs and wrote about them in this book.

After reading Dr. van Lommel's book, I was left with no doubt at all there is an existence after this physical life we experience is over. There is a part of us that goes on after we die. I guess we have to experience it to find out where our soul goes, but of this I am certain: it goes somewhere. There are too many instances of people having similar experiences when they die and are brought back to life by today's medical technology. Many of these people are able to describe what took place in the operating room where they died, things they couldn't possibly know. A person sees the location where a doctor misplaced an ink pen during an NDE and points it out to him at a later time. People describe conversations that took place while they were dead to the point of actually being able to point out who made the statements. All of these instances and more were described in detail and witnessed by others. I am beginning to find the more I read about such subjects, the less afraid of death I am and the more encouraged I am concerning death being merely a transition from one place to another.

Having spent a two- to three-year period absorbed in reading so many books, I found myself needing to dig even deeper into the subjects I had read about. My curiosity was aroused, and I felt the need for more answers. Given my previous research, I couldn't overlook the matter of psychics and mediums. I had become a fan of John Edward's television shows and books. I even attended one of his live shows in Portland, Maine. Since it was impossible at the time to get a private reading with him, I began to search out a tested psychic close to our home. I had this undeniable need to see if it was really real. One of our favorite sayings in Vietnam was, "It's okay, it's not really real." Strange the things that seem to stick close in our minds.

A friend referred me to a psychic in Kentucky she had been to. This friend told me that during a reading, the psychic told her she would give birth to a baby girl.

She told the psychic, "My tubes were tied, and I do not plan on any more children." She had the surgery performed after her last child to ensure just that.

The psychic said, "All I can tell you is what I see, and I see the birth of a baby girl in your future."

Eleven months later, my friend gave birth to a baby girl, her first after three boys. I became very interested and wanted to attend a reading, so I made an appointment. When you call this psychic's office, they only want your first name and no other information. I also called from a cell phone that doesn't show up on caller ID. Because they didn't ask for a lot of personal information which they could use to find out things about me before my visit, I went with an open mind and a curious attitude.

Shortly after sitting down and finishing the introductions, she told me I had been sick but I was healing now. She correctly said that I had an issue with my blood. I guess blood cancer is close enough to make it fit. We, or I should say she, talked for forty-five minutes. Although she was correct in much of what she said, I will share the details of just two of the more amazing items of interest.

She said, "I have a strange question. Who is a man called Ruby in your past? I see him as distantly related. He says you have something of his in your house?"

I was floored. Ruby was my great uncle Ruben's nickname, and I had a five-board bench in our living room that he made in the late 1800's, which we used as a plant stand. There was no way she could know these things. Maybe if she had more time and a lot more data, she could have searched my ancestry, but she had neither. I was amazed and the speed in which my belief system was being changed was accelerating rapidly.

I was seeing and reading too much evidence to believe otherwise. There is something else out there. There is a lot we do not know about the universe, but I am beginning to get glimpses of it, and I really love the peace this information is bringing me. I suppose this is what I am hoping you will do if you are facing your own mortality. Read, discover, learn, question others and yourself, and most of all, do not focus on negatives but look instead for something which gives you hope.

The last thing the psychic told me was that I would author a book, and the book would teach many people. I actually laughed out loud about that revelation. I had absolutely no intention of writing a book, nor did I feel I had the talent to write. Now, several years later, here you are reading it. I say that is strangely interesting!

The final book I will discuss in depth is one by Gary E. Schwartz, PhD, titled *The Energy Healing Experiments: Science Reveals Our Natural Power to Heal.* Dr. Schwartz received his PhD from Harvard University and was a professor of psychiatry at Yale University. He also was the Director of the Yale Psychophysiology Center. He is now a professor of psychology, medicine, neurology, psychiatry, and surgery at the University of Arizona. In other words, he is a well-educated man. The book is a study of energy healing, consciousness, and the mind's ability to heal disease. There are chapters that document successful attempts to measure energy transfer from the healer to another person. He also studies mediums and their ability to see things which are not visible to the rest of us. The book contains an in-depth study on what we can see with our eyes and what actually exists that we cannot see, and it does all of this in a very convincing manner.

Does Dr. Schwartz have his detractors? The answer is yes! There are people who take issue with every author I mention in this book. That is the way of the world. Everyone has his or her beliefs. What you should focus on is having an open mind during your personal search for hope and look at everything out there. As I have said before, if there has been a documented miracle for one person, there can be one for anyone searching for their own miracle.

I cannot begin to list all of the books I have read that have given me hope and led me to a new belief system. Since my journey started, I have read hundreds of books on several spiritual topics and can truthfully say

I became stronger spiritually through each of them. I've loved authors like Caroline Myss, PhD, who wrote *Anatomy of the Spirit* and *Defy Gravity* and many other wonderful books. Another favorite author is Dr. Wayne Dyer. He has written several books, and I have read all of them, including *The Shift* and *There's a Spiritual Solution to Every Problem*. Lastly, I read many books about Edgar Cayce, who gave readings from a trance state of mind concerning health issues, the past, and the future which were later found to be correct. One book I found especially informative was *The Edgar Cayce Remedies* by William A. McGarey, MD, a doctor who worked with Mr. Cayce. Beyond these books, you can research Hay House Publishing and Balboa Press for many more books about spirituality, hope and faith.

My favorite all-time author of fiction work is Stephen King. I have bought and read every book of his that has been published, with the exception of some limited-edition books, and I love the vacation my mind goes on when I am deeply wrapped up in one of his creative worlds. I have often said in somewhat a kidding manner that if Stephen King wrote notes on paper towels, I would purchase them for my reading pleasure. The non-fiction books I have mentioned above now have that same hold on me. These authors and more in this genre are moving, informative, inspirational, enlightened, and filled with passion for their beliefs. Their books are must reads for those of us in search of answers and hope.

There are also scores of videos you could watch that I found very inspiring, motivating, and informative. One in particular introduced me to several other people who would become central to my future longevity. The title of the movie (and book) is *The Secret,* by Rhonda Byrne. It is a movie explaining the Law of Attraction where "thoughts become things." There is a long list of people in the movie who explain the law. There are scientists, authors, philosophers, and leading spiritualists who give their views concerning positive thinking, gratitude, and attracting good things to yourself. People who have successfully used the Law of

Attraction give much evidence in this movie. I think the subject matter and the manner in which it is taught makes it a must-watch video and the book a good read.

The information is out there. Open your mind and read voraciously. Remember, knowledge is power, and with this power you can create change both within yourself and in your outside environment. If you can't read, have someone read to you or listen to audio books. Stay positive, shun negativity and negative people, listen to evidence, listen to your intuition, search for balance, and lastly fill yourself with hope. Remember this quote: "Hope never abandons you; you abandon it," by George Weinberg. Don't let hope disappear from your heart no matter what others say.

Chapter Four

Bumps in the Road to Recovery

T HIS WILL BE ONE OF the most difficult chapters in this endeavor for me to pen. The subject at hand is one I never wanted to experience and do not want to revisit, but sharing this part of me may ease the journey for someone else. My experience was something I now feel I must have been destined to have in order to continue to grow and understand my place in this universe. However, I didn't enjoy that it made me question my newfound positive mindset, my belief that anything is possible, and my faith that our bodies are powerful and capable of anything. I suppose, in the end, I realized I was not quite as evolved in thought and deed as I had believed myself to be.

One of the last things I told you in the previous chapter was to seek balance in all you do in your recovery. I wish I had known all along exactly how important a simple word like "balance" could be in the road to recovery. Brian Tracy said, "Just as your car runs more smoothly and requires less energy to go faster and farther when the wheels are in perfect alignment, you perform better when your thoughts, feelings, emotions, and values are in balance."

I had walked completely away from Western medicine for almost two years and totally dedicated myself to other healing modalities. And to be honest, I had done very well if you consider that the second doctor told me I would be very sick by November of 2008. I ate well. I slept well. I had energy. I worked a limited amount of time on the farm doing light chores. I rode the tractor. If I cut myself, I healed. I had a good relationship with my wife and son, and I was not depressed. I felt as if I was in a good place all around.

As it turns out, I should have looked at the whole picture and realized there were some things that Western medicine could help with to ensure a long lasting healing. The anger that initially felt so good clouded my judgment somewhat and allowed my ego to rule my actions. Now I believe shedding yourself of a strong ego is beneficial to your long-term health. If only I knew earlier in this experience how important it would be to my healing process, maybe the outcome would have been less painful.

The particular disease I was diagnosed with has several rather nasty sides to it, one of which is it erodes your bones. It causes lytic lesions, or rather large spots on your bones where bone matter is lost, and this erosion weakens the structure of the bones. It usually occurs in the long bones of your body but can happen anywhere. Early in the third year after my diagnosis, I broke my first rib. I remember when it happened because the pain was the most intense I had ever experienced.

Trust me, even though I have never given birth (in this life time, anyway), I have had kidney stones, so I do know a little about pain. The pain from the broken rib was extreme. It happened when I was throwing a bale of hay. I guess the twisting action and the weight of the hay was enough to snap a rib that had been partially eaten away. X-rays revealed the break, and I was told it would take about six weeks to heal. I couldn't wear anything to assist with the pain because wraps would restrict my breathing and could cause pneumonia. There wasn't much I could do but wait, not cough, and not lift anything heavy. If only things were that easy.

When I was almost at the end of the six-week healing process, I caught a cold, and it was a wicked booger. I coughed almost nonstop but otherwise was managing the cold and not running any fever. Then I broke rib number two during a violent coughing fit. I didn't know this at the time, but even a healthy person can break a rib while coughing, so for someone already compromised, breaking it turned out to be exceptionally easy. I didn't realize at the time how dangerous things had suddenly become and that we were actually just beginning a perilous downward spiral.

Having a cold and a broken rib created an environment in my body for pneumonia to take residence. I couldn't cough deeply because of the pain, so I couldn't rid my body of the mucus in my lungs and bad things happened. I went to one of the few Western medical professionals I felt I could trust. She wanted to immediately admit me to a hospital, and I refused. Once again, my ego got in the way of my healing. But it was a reaction to fear more than anger. I was so afraid of being told once again I was going to die that I could not put my care in the hands of those who offered no hope. The fear was palpable and overwhelming. The bitterness that accompanied the fear was akin to biting into a lime while expecting the taste of a ripe peach; it was like nothing I had ever felt before.

Antibiotics, inhalers, and a great many other temporary healing aids accompanied me home. In due time, I returned to good or, I should say, comparatively good health. I had lost some weight, and it took a while for my appetite to return, but I did feel much better. My ribs had healed, and the only reminder was occasional twinges of pain.

Then in rapid succession I broke ribs number three and four. Still I did not seek help from any Western medical professional. Anger and ego ruled my thought process even while I was trying to be a peaceful and enlightened person. I supposed it is obvious to you that I hadn't learned much about "balance" yet. A short while after the fourth rib fractured, I faced my most challenging problem to date, and it turned out to be the one that would chart my course for a long time to come.

Unknown to me, a vertebra in my thoracic spine had also been eroded due to the unchecked progression of this problem, and in June of 2010, I broke my spine. I knew *when* it happened, but I didn't know *what* had happened. I thought I had broken another rib. When you break a bone like I had, you feel it vibrate throughout your chest cavity. I felt the same immediate intense pain as I did when the fractured ribs snapped, but this time was a little different. The pain was even more intense and radiated across my chest like a searing, electric shock. I lived with this pain until October of 2010 without seeking any intervention. This time, the fear almost cost me my mobility.

My mindset being what it was, I spent the summer much like I always had; the only difference was the amount of pain I was in. Jennifer found a type of brace that I could wrap around my chest, and it would alleviate some of the pain. We vacationed in Gettysburg and Maine. We kayaked, rode four-wheelers, and swam. There were times when I had to crawl on my hands and knees to get somewhere, but I still did not seek medical help. It wasn't until my posture changed dramatically and my spine gave the appearance of being somewhat buckled that I relented.

In October 2010, I had an MRI. The next day I received a phone call telling me I had an appointment with a spine surgeon the next morning, which was a Friday. I thought that was a very quick appointment and figured the doctor couldn't be very busy if he could see me that fast. Jennifer was with me the next morning when we kept the appointment.

Dr. Richard Holt entered the examination room with a chart in his hands. I was standing because it helped lessen the pain, and Jennifer was sitting. Dr. Holt looked at us, looked at his chart, and promptly left the room.

He returned within a couple of minutes and asked, "Are you Richard Rowland?"

I answered, "Yes, I am."

He then said, "I thought I had the wrong room; you are supposed to be paralyzed." He went on to explain that most of the vertebra that had broken was gone and what was left had compressed my spinal cord by one-third. He showed us the image made by the MRI, and for the first time, I felt fear for me instead of fear of a doctor's negative prophecies.

I must say, even through all of this trial, I have always admired surgeons above all others in the medical field, followed closely by emergency/trauma physicians. I see them as people who fix something that is broken, as mechanics for the body as opposed to those who suck hope, fill you with fear, and try to keep you on prescription medicines. As it turned out, Dr. Holt was a well-respected surgeon with years of experience and one of the few doctors in Kentucky who could do this surgery successfully. It was Friday, and surgery was scheduled for Monday, just two days later. I closed my eyes and finally realized just how dangerous my refusal to seek and accept help had been during the past four months.

After the five-hour surgery to replace the vertebra with a cadaver bone, install two rods with assorted hardware, and a two-day stay at the hospital, I left early on Wednesday morning to go home. I was supposed to stay at the hospital seven to ten days. However, when I regained consciousness from the anesthesia, I asked how soon I could leave. I was told, "When you can walk fifty feet." I walked fifty feet with a walker the next day and was released soon after I accomplished that feat. I didn't fight to leave because of hardheadedness but because I firmly believe that the quicker you leave a hospital, the better your chance of survival. I also believe it reduces your chance of catching something else that could compromise you even more.

Poor Jennifer was taxed with caring for an invalid, and a hardheaded one at that, but she rose to the challenge and kept me in check. I sincerely appreciate her and our son for taking on everything at the house, farm, and business, as well as looking after my needs while I recovered. Dr. Holt called me his star patient! My attitude, assistance from family, drive to get better, and faith in my future pushed me to improve daily. I fully intended to beat all the odds, to live for a long time yet, to prove the experts wrong, and to be the first person diagnosed with this disease to attain a permanent remission.

I was released from Dr. Holt's care a year after the surgery. I still had room for improvement, but I was nowhere near as weak and ailing as I had been the previous October. As I reached the two-year anniversary of the surgery, I still continued to improve. Yes, I can tell you when changes in the weather are approaching. I am uncomfortable every day, and I live with some pain on a daily basis, but none of that compares to the pain I experienced before the surgery.

During my recovery from the spine surgery, I spent a large portion of my time gnawing on thoughts concerning my health and the steps I needed to undertake in order to improve my chances of sticking around a bit longer. I had developed a real fear that bordered on panic of suffering another fracture, and I had to relent and seek help from Western medicine.

I made another appointment at the veteran's hospital (VA) in Louisville to seek the assistance of a hematology/oncology specialist. I wanted someone who would be conservative in thought and someone who would let me partner in my own health, and I definitely did not want the doctor I saw in September of 2008. I did not think I could take her negativity. My thinking was the VA sees several cases of multiple myeloma because of its connection with Vietnam veterans, and that meant they should have experience treating it.

In a VA setting, you see residents or fellows, and they are supervised by a specialist in the field. I must say I met a good one this time. While first admitting this was an incurable disease and it would eventually be the cause of my demise, he was hopeful and described the disease as treatable for a good while in some cases. Many people do die within the first three years of diagnosis, but others can live a long time with newly developing treatments. He felt I would be in the "long-lasting" category, and so did I. He also admitted that a positive attitude would go a long way toward helping this endeavor succeed.

We agreed on a six-month run of a prescription medication which sometimes brings about a long-term remission. I also agreed to monthly infusions of a bone-building and—strengthening medication that would help prevent future fractures. These medications were not without possible dangerous side effects, but I put every ounce of positive thought, prayer, energy healing, and guided meditation I could muster into the belief that I would not experience any lasting problems while taking the medication. I am happy to say I experienced very few problems during the time I was taking the treatments.

Continuing the upbeat news, the markers in my blood that they look at when judging the progression of this particular disease first halted and then greatly reduced in number, to the point where further treatment other than the bone builder was not needed. I was to be observed only. I have monthly infusions and quarterly blood tests to check my status, but otherwise I am doing much better. I am weak at times during the day, but when that happens I take a nap and feel rejuvenated afterwards. Hell, I am over sixty years old; I have earned an afternoon nap if I want one.

Not everyone has such good success with their first treatment plan. Why was I different? I firmly believe that it helps to have a doctor who encourages you to be hopeful and to believe in your dreams and expectations, a doctor who believes in the ability of the mind, body, and spirit to assist with healing. I feel that having my earlier beliefs revitalized and renewed helped immensely. I also strongly believe doctors should focus on every person's quality of life and partner with them to insure they live, eat, and play well. Having a doctor who could accept that I would not obey doctor's orders solely because they were issued was also extremely helpful in this process.

I welcomed my doctor's advice, but I did not remove myself from the partnership and allow people to order me around. This is my body and my life, and I will always partake in the decision-making process concerning any treatment. It is through this partnership that I receive information and advice, then research it and listen to my intuition before making a decision. I believe spirituality is alive, that miracles are not only possible but they happen every day, and that I am going to beat this crisis with the plan I am practicing. And finally, I think accepting balance in all things was the most important step I had taken so far in this journey.

I am reminded of an old joke. There was a middle-aged man in his doctor's office. The doctor told him, "Frank, you have some problems going on with your body that are beyond my expertise to treat. Your blood test indicates I need to send you to a specialist so he can investigate further. I am afraid this could be serious, but let's look into it before worrying too much." Well, Frank was a very religious man and wanted to go home and pray on the matter and told his doctor just that. Frank prayed relentlessly for over a month. One day his doctor, being worried about Frank, called him to ask if he had decided to see the specialist. Frank said, "No doctor, I have been praying, and I believe my prayers are going to be answered."

Needless to say, a couple of weeks later Frank died and made his trip to the other side. When he arrived, he was overjoyed at the continuation of his existence but had a question for the Creator. Frank said, "God, although I am happy to be here, I prayed to you to heal me and let me remain on earth where I was also happy. Being a faithful man, why did you not grant my wish?" The Creator sighed and said, "Frank, not once but twice, I sent a specialist to cure you, and you declined the help. What more did you want me to do?" I guess the moral of the story is that the help is out there. You just need to keep looking until you find the right fit for you.

Why did I have to travel full circle to get to this point? Because I was filled with anger and fear, and I was egotistical. My advice to you if facing the same or similar challenges in your life is this: Like me, get a second opinion. Unlike me, if you don't like that one, don't walk away. Get a third or fourth opinion or as many as necessary to find the peace of mind you seek. Be a partner—and I mean a full partner—in your health. Do your research. Be knowledgeable about the disease you are diagnosed with and do not be afraid to speak up if you have questions. You will be respected if you do.

Chapter Five

The Limitations of Allopathic Medicine and the Effect of Environmental Issues

Allopathic medicine is a biologically or science-based approach to the practice of treating disease and the symptoms of disease. In simple terms, if you have a disease or its symptoms, there should be a pill to treat it. Allopathy looks for one part of a plant that may be helpful and synthesizes it to make a pill. Others might look instead at the plant's healing properties as a whole. The main opposites of allopathy are homeopathy and naturopathy. Allopathic medicine came to be in the 1800s with the discovery of new drugs and the birth of the American Medical Association (AMA).

How does this information fit in this book? Because I believe things have gotten completely out of balance. Hippocrates is generally considered to be the father of medicine, and he said, "Let food be your medicine and medicine be your food." He knew even back then that the power to heal and the causes of disease come from what you put in your mouth or otherwise absorb into your body. For years, the treatments of diseases were natural in character and many still could be today. That is not to say I oppose taking any so-called maintenance drugs or taking an antibiotic for the treatment of a bacterial infection; I have done both and would do so again if necessary. I do think you should make decisions regarding your treatment for medical issues from an informed state. Take notice of what is out there, and look at the different healing modalities that exist.

Western medicine is not the only thing to cling to when you need help. There are osteopaths, naturopaths, homeopaths, herbalists, chiropractors, and many other practices worth your time to investigate. And yes, you do have time to study and become knowledgeable. The time you spend exploring may well extend your life. Besides, I firmly believe the power to heal resides within your mind, body, and spirit. Evolving to the level required to harness this power is the trick. As I have said before, documentations of true medical miracles are out there. If a miracle can happen for one person, then it makes sense to believe it is possible for all people to experience the same joyful outcome. Seek knowledge with an open mind and you may just find the magic you are looking for.

I long for the days when doctors could be open minded about all the different ways to treat ailing people. Those were the days before civil litigation, insurance settlements, malpractice insurance, health insurance, being ruled by the AMA, people demanding a pill for everything, drug representatives, government controls, hungry lawyers, and lastly the proliferation of television, radio, and print advertisements.

The ability of doctors to treat based upon their training, beliefs, and research has been taken away by the AMA, along with the Federal Drug Administration (FDA) and the pharmaceutical companies. My belief and the belief of many people I talk to is that doctors have to treat based upon the guidelines of the AMA or lose their license to practice medicine. The FDA has woefully failed in its responsibility by not researching natural cures and by approving some drugs too quickly, only to be required to remove them later or issue warnings because of harmful side effects.

Pharmaceutical companies and the FDA live in the same house while renting the basement to the AMA. The three of them have made it almost impossible for a researcher with a possible natural cure to have the ability to make it through the trial phase because of the tremendous cost involved in doing so and the hoops they must jump through bureaucratically. No one in the allopathic side of medicine seems to be interested in natural cures because naturally occurring products cannot be patented; therefore drug companies cannot make massive amounts of money from them. Also, healthy people do not spend money on prescription drugs. If people were cured of diseases, drug companies would be out of business. Money is once again the motivator for a business, but then again it has to be in order to satisfy stockholders and make more money. Can you see the ditch being cut by the feet of a dinosaur walking in circles?

I have many thoughts concerning advertising, especially on television. I do not believe drug companies should be able to advertise on television. I should not have to explain to a child who happens to be watching television with me what erectile dysfunction is, what an erection is, or what those people in the commercial are in the mood to do. The subject of sex should be between parents and children, and the conversation should not be instigated by information viewed on a television set. Advertising should be placed where medical professionals could see it and research the data. Doctors should not be in the position of giving or denying a prescription to a patient based upon patient demand; the decision to prescribe should come from the doctor's knowledge and expertise. Just think about the massive amount of money spent by drug companies on advertising yearly and you will no longer wonder why prescription drugs are so expensive.

Through my research and reading I have developed a fervent belief that there are two motivators in life: fear and love. Everything we do starts with those two motivations. If only we could evolve to the point where fear is removed and we are motivated only by love. Doctors treat while motivated by the fear of being sued. Medical professionals over-treat and over-test in order to cover themselves in case they are wrong about something or, in some cases, to make more money. Hospitals and other medically related businesses (and yes, they are businesses) love it when doctors order tests because they make more money, and the bottom line in medicine is money.

Please do not make any mistake about it—medicine is big business. Look at the short list: doctors, specialists, x-ray technicians, pharmacists, pharmaceutical companies, FDA, AMA, DEA, local health departments, hospitals, rehabilitation hospitals, nursing homes, researchers of all kinds, rehabilitation therapy centers, medical schools, trade schools, nurses, nurse practitioners, certified nurse assistants, medical transcriptionists, maintenance people, janitorial personnel, laboratory technicians, attorneys, secretaries, medical assistants, respiratory therapists, and the list could go on. They are motivated by money and in business because the fear of death and illness is *your* motivator. They instill that fear into you in different ways. If you don't do this, you might die. Take this or you will never get better. We have just the pill to make you feel better. You might get cancer, or have a heart attack, or hell, you might just break out in black, yellow, and purple stripes, but take this pill and look good for a while like the people on this commercial who are probably actors and have never really had this disease.

Then there are the actors on television pretending to be trusted doctors sincerely delivering messages while wearing the blue or white jacket with the stethoscope draped over their shoulder. Never mind that if they used one they wouldn't have any idea what they were listening to or for. As long as it looks cool and professional, they will wear it. They sincerely want you to hear about this new drug that is the answer to your prayers. What they really want is to be paid for making the commercial. Whatever happened to truth in advertising? It brings to mind the fact you rarely see heavyset or obese people in fast food commercials, even though if that is where you eat regularly, chances are you are going to gain weight. Instead they show thin, healthy-looking people having a good time eating. I have been in these places, and this is not what I see. To me, this method of advertising is not unlike the snake oil salesmen of old; it's just a newer version.

If you have insurance or money, you are loved and the treatment is there for you until you max out on one or the other. Then you move into the pool of people who have neither and may not receive the top care available. I have seen doctors visit patients in a hospital setting by simply sticking their head in the door and asking the patient "How are you today?" They leave after the answer and bill the insurance company for a hospital visit. I sometimes wonder just how many patients they might visit a day in this same manner and what the expense is to patients and insurance companies. I have also seen patients kept in a hospital until the insurance was exhausted, only to then be shipped to a rehabilitation hospital because insurance would once again pay for treatment. Only when it all runs out are they sent home.

During an emergency room visit once, tests were ordered that would have cost our insurance company thousands of dollars as well as hundreds of dollars in co-pays that we would have been responsible for. We felt the tests were not necessary and refused them, only to be labeled as uncooperative and going against medical advice. In the end, a fifteen-dollar visit to the family doctor and a ten-dollar lab test revealed a kidney/bladder infection. The MRI, CAT scan, x-rays, and blood tests were not needed because a simple urinalysis found the problem. Why can't Western medicine start with the simplest, least invasive, and safest test and go from there if the answer isn't apparent? What happened to the oath "First, do no harm?" After all, too much radiation over your lifetime will harm you. Once again, treatment is money driven, and you agree to certain treatments from a position of instilled fear instead of a place of educated calm.

As you can see, I sometimes get very passionate about the injustices I observe and want people to see the things I have witnessed firsthand.

I am disappointed by health care in this country and by the inability of those in power to look at the whole picture without factoring in money. I guess the things I wrote above are indicative of just that mindset.

We patients need to take credit for part of the problem as well. Have you ever given consideration to the possibility that just maybe we are sick because our bodies can no longer handle the toxins we eat, breathe, and absorb? Do you remember the earlier analogy about the water glass that can only hold so much before it overflows? Let's see, scientists have introduced foreign DNA into plants and genetically modified them in order to make them produce more food. We introduce substances into our bodies that have no business being there, such as herbicides, insecticides, and petroleum-based fertilizers. We breathe in air saturated with foreign particles generalized as smog. We absorb radiation from all kinds of electronic devices, including the computer I am currently typing on in order to write this book. We drink water that is contaminated with agricultural runoff, prescription drugs, industrial pollutants, sewage, and a poison called fluoride.

And we do all of this willingly because the FDA says that the toxins are at safe levels for human use or consumption. This is the same FDA who has approved drugs which are later revealed to cause cancer, heart disease, and other life-ending disorders. Have we really become that willing to let ourselves be led by government? Is there any wonder that one out of every four people will be diagnosed with cancer? It no longer surprises me.

Cancer used to be relatively rare, yet it has grown to unmanageable proportions in relation to other diseases. Cancer touches all of us, and the incidence of diagnosis is certainly a rapidly rising occurrence. We need to be careful that we don't get to the point where we allow its commonness to dull our compassion. Whether people live a long time after being diagnosed or succumb quickly, we need to keep them and their families in our daily thoughts and prayers.

The FDA would love to get total control of the vitamin and supplement business in this country. There have been studies published about some vitamins and supplements being dangerous for you or of them not being beneficial. Look closely and you will see that most of these studies are focused on synthetic, man-made, laboratory-tweaked and—developed vitamins and supplements. They get in the body and attempt to mimic what real food does for you. Synthetics will never accomplish what real food and whole-food vitamins and supplements can as they relate to your body.

Take for instance vitamin C. The commercially produced and cheaply priced vitamin C is ascorbic acid, which is only one part of the actual makeup of natural vitamin C. There are several things in natural vitamin C that you do not get by taking only one part, and when you do that you get things out of balance. There is that word once again.

Is this just a problem without a solution? If that were the case, I would not have wasted my time writing about it. I believe one of the many reasons I have been able to keep this disease at bay is a major change in my diet. We eat, grow, can, preserve, dry, and freeze organic fruits, vegetables, and herbs. We fertilize with compost that we make right here. We filter fluoride, lead, and chlorine out of our water. We buy local produce from farmers' markets. The limited amount of meat we eat is grass fed as well as being hormone, steroid, and antibiotic free. Our eggs are locally produced in a free-range environment and fed organically. We also make our own bread with organically grown ingredients.

Jennifer makes all of our lye-based soaps with organic essential oils. Think about this for a moment. You are bathing or showering in hot water that opens your pores, and then you are rubbing a bar of chemical-packed soap on your skin which then soaks into the pores. To top it off, you jump out of the shower and apply an antiperspirant that usually contains aluminum. Five years ago, we started using deodorant stones that last for years in order to limit the metals we knowingly absorb into our bodies.

By doing the things I listed above and more, I still believe my glass will inevitably fill once again, but it will fill at a much slower rate than the glass of someone who doesn't change what he or she ingests. I also realize that the practices listed above would be very challenging for commercial agriculture to utilize and still feed all of the people in this world like they do today with the methods they currently employ. However, I am talking about you and I and the fact that we are facing our own challenges medically. In order for us to prolong our lives and still have a good quality of life, we must change what we do. Perhaps a quote often attributed to Albert Einstein says it best, "Insanity is doing the same thing over and over again but expecting different results." If you want to heal yourself or be a major player in the team that is trying to heal your body, change what you did that got you where you are.

Let me leave you with three simple words of advice before closing this chapter; investigate, explore, and study. Did you notice they are synonyms? Do your homework concerning whatever challenges your health and longevity. Make your decisions based upon the answers you find.

As a case in point, when I returned to Western medicine to explore treatments, my kidney function was failing because of the excessive levels of protein my kidneys were forced to filter. The initial dosage of the drug I had agreed to take for six months was lowered because it was felt my kidneys could not handle the added burden. Unknown to my doctors, which I do not recommend, Jennifer contacted an herbalist who suggested a kidney flush weekly. I started that process immediately. My kidney function returned to normal within the first month and has stayed there ever since.

After that one month, the dosage was increased to what the doctors wanted me to take originally. I can still remember how pleasantly surprised they were that my kidney function returned. I am still not sure if my doctor would have agreed with me taking the herb mixture, but my research and intuition told me to do it anyway. I think now I should have discussed it with him after the improvement was noticed, but I still have not. As a stated before, I do not recommend you keep secrets from the doctor you employ. I should have just been up front and stood my ground concerning my decision about my body. Remember it is your body, not theirs.

You must change the things that brought you to your current place of worry. Most importantly, believe there are differences you can make, because I promise you, a new you resides in your old shell.

Chapter Six

When the Conclusion Isn't the End

THIS CHAPTER OF *UNSPOKEN MESSAGES* was relatively easy to bring to life in written form. The chapter and the title have been in the file drawers I create in my mind since this venture started, waiting for the proper time to pull them out and transfer the thoughts to words. Many of the people who have had conversations with me during the past five years will see familiar phrases written among these pages. Words I spoke to them that were wrapped in belief and absolute certainty will look very recognizable. They have lived inside me for so long they are now a large part of the person the new me has become. Maybe that is why cancer survivors count two birthdays. I have the anniversary of my birth in October of each year, which gives a count of my chronological age, and then there is the anniversary of my diagnosis, which now totals five-plus years and counting.

In this chapter I will delve into what I now believe about our continued existence and immortality and why I believe the things I have come to embrace without reservation. But, before taking this thread of thought through the needle's eye in my mind and stitching this tale together, I must give you the best advice I can possibility manage to convey to others who share this journey with me. I believe very powerfully in these messages, and if your intuition led you to read this book, know that I cannot state strongly enough the importance of the timeliness of the message when conveying these thoughts to you.

You must first forgive yourself for any wrong you consider yourself to have committed. This will not be easy, because you probably do not feel deserving of forgiveness, but it is the most important step in the healing process. The power of regret is a burden much like a yoke would be if wrapped around your neck; it weighs you down and keeps you rooted in a fertile plot that allows disease to grow unabated. The disease will show up physically, emotionally, or mentally, but show up it will. I am now well past middle age and without a doubt have carried wishes and regrets around with me from the past. I have residing inside me things I wish I hadn't done, things I did that were wrong and I knew it, people I have hurt, times I was untruthful, things I wish I had done differently, and too many wrongs to possibly list.

You have a list of things inside you too. You are a human being, and you have made mistakes; it is part of the growing and learning we all go through. Go on, look inside yourself, gaze in the mirror, and you will know that I am not the only one to have regrets for actions of the past. Every one of you has secrets you would just as soon take to the grave with you. The problem is those secrets may very well carry you there much sooner than you'd like if you do not release their hold on you. Perhaps Roberto Assagioli said it best when he stated, "Without forgiveness, life is governed by an endless cycle of resentment and retaliation." Break the cycle and allow yourself to forgive yourself first; then you have taken the first step to healing.

The act of forgiveness brings about a change within you, and there are many methods you can employ in order to forgive yourself. You might choose to write the things you need forgiveness for on a sheet of paper and then set the paper on fire and let the words disappear in smoke. You could type them on a computer and then delete them or record them on a CD and then destroy the recording. Use your imagination and be creative. Close your eyes and envision the imagined wrongs being encased in a bubble, and then just let it float away. All of these methods are mentioned in many of the books I have read over the past five years. This is your chance to have a much needed re-do or re-boot. It is the birth of a new you and a chance to let go of the past, but you must be sincere about cutting the chains binding you to your history and creating an environment conducive to good health instead of disease given birth by regret.

The next step is to ask forgiveness from those you believe you have wronged and those who have mistreated you. It doesn't matter whether they grant forgiveness or choose to continue to harbor resentment. The important point is you asked, and by doing so, you rid your mind, body, and spirit of the inner turmoil you have been holding on to. If contacting them is not possible, try using the methods listed above, symbolically receiving the forgiveness you desire.

You must stop living in the past and start living in the now. Once you rid yourself of the yoke you have been carrying, you can go forward a lighter and wiser person. Try to live a more spiritual life but know you will continue to have moments of failure. All of us do unless we have evolved spiritually to the same level as Jesus, Buddha, Muhammad, Mahatma Gandhi, His Holiness the Dalai Lama, Desmond Tutu, Mother Teresa, or some other extremely enlightened soul.

When you do have setbacks, forgive yourself immediately instead of allowing negative thoughts to once again gain a foothold in your mind and accumulate. Many of the books I have read point to the belief that your mind can create illness in your body if left unchecked. Your mind can also assist in healing whatever illness plagues you. Take control of the rest of your life, find your faith no matter what it is in, and believe without doubt miracles can occur in your life.

When I unwillingly started this journey, I decided to look upon it as an investigation for the truth, a search for what is real, and an exploration of what is possible. I must admit in the beginning I was somewhat skeptical of anything new and not science based, or science that was not mainstream in nature, as well as anything not normal to my life's previous experience. I have grown into a person who believes in many different things, a person who finally has evolved into someone wiser and more accepting of unknown mysteries, someone much happier than I was before.

When I first started reading the genre of books and watching movies filled with spirituality, healings, and miracles, I read that some people look upon a cancer diagnosis as a blessing. I thought to myself this is a blessing I could do without in my life. But as I have moved along, I find I must agree with them. If not for this diagnosis, I would have never made the discoveries I have been blessed to experience. I would not have grown into the much more caring, loving, and compassionate person I have become, and I love my newfound deep appreciation for others and what they mean to me. Instead, I would still be the curmudgeon of old, a role I was very comfortable with at the time.

So yes, a cancer diagnosis has been a blessing in my life, and the old me would have never thought that possible. I have become very comfortable in my skin knowing there is a part of me which will continue on even after I am no longer using this body. The old me believed it was very possible immortality meant nothing more than your memory living on in others after you die.

Saying I am convinced we are immortal is such a vast understatement that it doesn't begin to convey the depth of my belief in what I have come to see as an absolute truth. It is akin to saying the Bible is merely a book or true love is simply a shared emotion. I am not just convinced. I am certain, one hundred percent sure, absolutely positive without a grain of doubt, the death of the shell containing your soul or energy is just a simple transition from one plane to another. The absolute answer to what and where this plane is located still eludes me. Is it heaven? Is it a parallel universe? Does your soul travel to another entirely different universe? Do you shoot through wormholes into spaces and places unknown to us right now? Do we evolve and become spirit guides for the living? Does our energy hover around this world, unseen by others?

Does our soul take a short break only to reincarnate into another being of some sort or another with new lessons to learn? I feel the answer is a resounding *yes*. It may just be we do all of those things and more. Now there is an idea worth exploring!

Deepak Chopra, a leader in the field of mind/body medicine, brought up another possibility to think about. What if everything you see, touch, feel, hear, and smell is your creation, and you are the main energy driving the universe? At the time I read his book, the idea was difficult for me to fathom. Now it has become another on the list of vast possibilities. I wish I had the answers and could let you in on the biggest secret of all time, but I have not solved the riddle of life. However, this I can say with emphatic sureness: we do continue on in some other state of being when we are finished using the current shell in which we live.

The investigative mind I possess is sure of this because I have found so much evidence indicating there is much more to this life than appears on the surface. Science has mapped out only 5 percent of our DNA and calls the other 95 percent "junk" DNA. Just because we do not yet understand something doesn't mean it does not exist or have a purpose in our conscious existence. After all, at one time it was thought tonsils and the appendix had no useful purpose. Now it is known they both play a vital role in the immune system. When titling this chapter, I strived to have a heading which conveyed my absolute belief that life of some sort continues after the death of the body, and the title *When the Conclusion Isn't the End* seemed to fit perfectly. Our body's life may end, but it is not the conclusion of our existence.

I believe intuition is not merely a feeling you experience but a message being sent to you. I wish I knew where the message originated. Could it be from the Creator, angels, spirit guides, the universe, our energy, or from an infinite number of other possibilities? I don't know yet, but I feel it is important to listen to and act upon the intuitive messages you receive. My belief is not in randomness but in a master plan of some sort and it has a purpose. The plan appears to be changeable and fluid under the right circumstances but without reservation I believe it exists.

That may be hard to swallow, with all the bad things seeming to happen to the species inhabiting this earth, but keep this in mind when thinking about all the dreadful ways beings on this earth are killed or die: this may just not be the end. Start with the word "may" as you think about death. What if I am right, and death is a transition or a homecoming that you just do not remember experiencing before and you will actually feel glorious after the trip? If this is the case, you will no longer worry about the loved ones you left behind because in actuality, you will not have left anyone. All souls, all energy, are eventually reunited once again. I often think of one of my favorite quotes when I meet new people with whom I feel an immediate shared kinship. I'm not sure who said it first, but it goes like this: "My soul has known your soul for a long time." Have you ever had an instance where you meet someone for what you think is the first time but it seems like you have known each other forever? Well, maybe you have! You may have been unknowingly searching for each other, and intuition may have led you to meet again.

When I met Jennifer, it was just one of those moments. I had been divorced for three years and retired from the state police for a year. A friend of mine who still worked for the state police called me one night. I had just started a horse stabling and training business and was new to this part of the trade.

He said, "I have a lady here that is traveling. She has been on the road all day. She's tired and needs a place to board her horse overnight so she can get some rest."

I told him, "I do not board horses overnight because they can unknowingly bring diseases to my farm and pass them on to other horses."

He said, "Come on, Richard, this is a nice lady, and she needs help."

I once again told him, "No, I am not going to board a horse overnight."

He then said, "Just a minute," and he handed her the phone, knowing full well I would not deny her the help she needed if I spoke to her.

My friend gave her an escort to the farm. From the very moment we met, I felt an intense attraction and an understanding that something special was happening. Her hands shook as she handed me the registration and health certificates for her horse, and mine shook so much that I looked at the papers but couldn't seem to take them from her. We knew, we just knew, this was supposed to be.

Prior to meeting Jennifer, I was convinced I would remain a bachelor, but that soon changed. We began a long-distance relationship, traveling to see each other occasionally, and she moved here a year later. I proposed to her in front of the barn where we had first met two years before, and we were married on horseback in front of the same barn a year later. We have been together this in this life for over twelve years, but we both know this isn't the first time nor will it be the last. To paraphrase the quote, I know my soul has known her soul for a long time.

My best friend in life is a very spry eighty-seven year old named Lee Durbin. That would make him twenty-five years older than me. We met over twenty years ago and have been best friends ever since that very moment in time. However, I really believe our friendship began many lifetimes ago.

I entered a restaurant one night to take a coffee break from patrolling. I had a favorite table I liked to sit at, and the waitresses would try to keep the table open for me. That particular night when I entered, I saw a man and a woman sitting where I would normally take my break. There were other tables I could have sat at, but I walked up to mine and, completely out of character for me, announced, "You are sitting at my favorite table, and that leaves me no choice but to join you." They both smiled, and a grand friendship began anew, one which would span many years.

We shared time on this earth and did many things together, including sharing the death of his beloved Ellie some years later. I was the only person she would allow to visit her when her time to leave became close, and her husband and I were the only people she would smile for, and a beautiful smile it was. He also accompanied me across country to bring the love of my life and her horse to their new home. Once again, I have no doubt my soul has known his soul for a long time.

Nothing is happenstance, and nothing happens by coincidence. In my mind, coincidence does not exist; nothing is luck, and almost everything that happens is supposed to happen just as it does. That being said, I believe you can attract certain possibilities with your mind and positive energy. I believe "attracting" to be part of the evolving and enlightening process we go through as we learn or remember who we really are inside the body we carry.

When I first started going to an energy healer, I felt I was staring at an eventual death, one which would occur sooner rather than later. I would get angry inside when she would say, "Everything is as it is supposed to be" or "It is what it is" or "Things are as they are." No matter how she worded it I wanted to fight it, because I did not want things to be as they are (were). I eventually learned acceptance moves you forward with more wisdom and happiness than defiance does.

That is not to say I do not mourn the self I was before this diagnosis changed my life because I still, to this day, experience a certain degree of longing when I think of the old life I used to live. However, I have learned we all reach a point in life where we must realize forward is the only direction, now is the only time, and change is the only constant. I have learned to embrace all I have, regardless of the title describing it, and I spend my time doing what makes me happy.

Finally, life has become about me, and it can be this way for you as well. A challenge like this has to partly be experienced alone, completely within you, without a guidebook to lead the way. Regardless of your attitude when beginning the journey, the end result will be inner growth and enlightenment. Keep in mind even though you travel the path alone, your gifts of intuition, the love of family, and the support of friendships will shore up the bridges you have yet to cross.

There are many books and movies that teach about the power of the Law of Attraction. Since the research is out there, I will only write a very basic explanation of the law. You can attract to you things you want in your life through absolute faith and believing you will receive them, maintaining positive energy, holding onto sincere feelings of gratitude before receiving whatever you desire, and a continuous focus upon that which you want, be it good health, relationships, riches, or anything else we humans desire in our lives. The books have many examples of how the Law worked just as they say it would.

I have used it myself with success but always with small things. Once, when going to the hospital to visit my friend, I told my wife, "There will be a parking place on the first level of the parking garage, on the right, two-thirds of the way up the incline." That would put us the closest to the entrance of the hospital. I used the law as taught and felt the gratitude flow out of my body. When we arrived, I found a parking place just exactly where I said I would. All the other parking places on the first level were occupied.

Sometimes when going to town and running late, I will say, "We will be on time because we will not catch any red lights." During those trips, we will not catch one single red light. There have been many more instances where I have had success using this belief. Coincidence? I do not believe in this word at all. Why then, you might ask, do I not use the law and rid myself of this diagnosis I carry around? The answer would be because of fear; fear of failure and the result of failure would be a questioning all of my newly held beliefs. So in reality, I lack of the level of faith I need for success.

Remember those two main motivators I spoke of earlier, fear and love? I have not yet evolved to the point of absolute faith and having love as the main motivator in my life. I find myself able to have faith in the small things and work the law to my benefit, but I can't master what it takes for the big items. This brings to mind the book *Conversations with God: An Uncommon Dialogue* by Neale Donald Walsch. In the book, he asked God for clarification on the subject of affirmation statements or the state of being filled with gratitude and appreciation for what you are about to receive. He wrote that God said, "Jesus had such clarity. Before every miracle, he thanked Me in advance for its deliverance. It never occurred to Him not to be grateful, because it never occurred to Him that what he declared would not happen. The thought never entered his mind." And such is the level of faith and belief I feel you need to attain in order to receive those things you pray for or wish to receive.

Think of it this way: Jesus walked on water because of absolute faith. The thought never crossed his mind he couldn't perform such a miracle. I admit I am not yet at that level but am merely traveling towards it with the knowledge the power exists and with absolute faith I can harness it, and you can too.

A very good friend who also happens to be a medical doctor had this suggestion concerning my fear of failure: "Maybe instead of taking the big step and wanting a cure all, you should coexist with the diagnosis and live to a ripe old age." I found it amazing that the statement came from a medical doctor. She believed the body, mind, and spirit are very powerful tools in healing, just as I do. Maybe, just maybe, there is a shift of thought occurring in this country, and there is hope for a new future where all aspects of healing are considered. My hope is this is an exciting time to be alive in the physical sense and people are seeing more of the vast layers of possibilities in existence. I am going to start a new thought process with the goal my doctor friend suggested, and I feel success awaiting me.

I believe you cannot change your circumstances by doing the same things that brought you to this place initially. If you are healthy mentally, spiritually, and physically, you probably don't need this advice, but if you find yourself in a deepening well of despair in the face of your mortality, stop traveling the same path and start a new journey. Start looking at old things in a new way. Don Henley and Stanley Lynch wrote a song some years ago that was recorded by the Eagles titled *Learn to Be Still*. I listen to this song when I feel the need to be centered after a rough day. I find the lyrics, "Now the flowers in your garden, they don't smell so sweet, so sweet. Maybe you've forgotten the heaven lying at your feet," extremely significant to the centering process.

Take a look around yourself every day and find something to be thankful for in its existence. Nature has painted a stunning display for your enjoyment, and it is available to you every day of your life. It is as simple as walking around your own heaven and seeing what has been there all along.

A peaceful Kentucky sunset over the stables, courtesy Richard D. Rowland

See it, really see it, maybe for the first time in a long time, and appreciate the nature around you for what it is, a gift to you from the Creator. Get out of your negative state of mind. Do something so completely different you will surprise yourself and others by your actions, and you will be astonished by the speed with which your mood changes for the better.

Stop focusing on death, dying, illness, the pain accompanies disease, and the fears of failure or abandonment swirling unendingly through your mind every day. You might just find yourself, upon retiring, sleeping a peaceful sleep, surrounded by softly felt dreams which dance lightly instead of the head-banging death knell of the Grim Reaper pounding on drums with a beat seeming to reverberate through your very soul.

What can you do differently? The famous Brazilian lyricist and novelist Paulo Coelho once said, "One day you will wake up and there won't be any more time to do all the things you've always wanted. Do it now." I wanted to dance with joy and laughter when I read those words and others like them. It was as if I could finally give myself permission to do all the things I always wanted to do, but maybe there was a part of me feeling self-conscious or silly about doing them in front of others. There used to be a part of me always saying, "What will others think?" The new me says, "To hell with what others think—how will it make me feel?" Finally, I am the one that matters the most. In order to love and love deeply, you must first love yourself completely. Quit holding back. As Coelho says, "Do it now."

I think everyone should have a renewable bucket list of things they want to do. As you complete the things on your list, add more, because there will always be more things you want to do before your time here is over. This is where I want to scream, "It's okay. It's not selfish and it's not childish to want your dreams fulfilled." Fulfill as many of your dreams as you can, and continue to dream as long as you live in this physical sphere. There is an old adage, "Live each day as if it were your last." I agree with that, but at the same time I say you should also live each day as if you were going to live forever.

Here's a case in point. Why does a person facing an imminent demise of their physical being need a new truck, need to finish a new bathroom in the basement, need a new implement for the tractor, need to make reservations for a vacation a year away, or need to start writing a book? Because I believe planning for a future, any future, may just ensure that you have a future.

There are books filled with examples of people who were supposed to die but instead lived to see certain goals met. So make goals, make plans, chase dreams, have a list of to-dos, and then do all of those things. When you finish, make another list. You want to go on a zip line? If you have the energy and it is going to make you feel good about life, go ride the line and scream at the top of your lungs with laughter. A lady in my community went zip lining for her eightieth birthday and had a great time, and you can too.

One of my favorite singer/songwriters is Jimmy Buffett. Yes, I am a Parrot-head from way back. In the lyrics of one of his songs, *Growing Older but Not Up,* he writes "I'd rather die while I'm living than live while I'm dead." I love the song, love the lyrics, and embrace the whole mindset. Don't live filled with thoughts of impending doom; live with wonder and childlike amazement at all surrounding you. The magic is there! Can you see it? We are all going to die someday, make no mistake about it. No one has ever made it out otherwise. While you are here, spend some time living and become confident when you do die, it will be a transition, not an end.

In the vein of doing something different and shaking my life up, I tried several unusual things—unusual to me, anyway. One of the items high on my list of things I wanted to experience was to go on a real ghost hunt. During the early stages after my diagnosis, that is exactly what I did. A good friend and fellow retired police officer had formed a paranormal group in the area and invited my wife and me to accompany them on an investigation. My now open mind was ready without a doubt to have this experience.

We met one beautiful summer evening filled with anticipation. The target of our investigation was a very old theater in our town which was being restored. Management and construction workers dubbed it a hotspot of paranormal activity. If you read publications concerning paranormal activity, you will see reports of an increase of experiences in older structures that are being restored or remodeled. There were five of us in the group, all armed with digital recorders, flashlights, and other items needed to participate in the investigation. Jennifer and I, being novices, only had flashlights, recorders, and one set of night vision goggles.

We entered the dark theater around 9:00 p.m. After receiving our instructions and other lists of do's and don'ts, we started performing a walk around in our assigned areas searching first for EVP's. EVP's are electronic voice phenomena, which can be noises and possibly voices you might not actually hear with your own senses but may possibly be captured on a recording device. What you would do is walk around asking questions and making statements, hoping you would be lucky enough to receive a response.

I was about forty yards from the nearest person, on the back part of the stage behind a curtain. It was incredibly dark, and the air felt very heavy. At the time, I remember wondering how much of what I was feeling was real or whether I was making it up because of anticipation of what might actually take place and the rush of adrenalin I was experiencing. I felt a little self-conscious asking questions into a recorder while no other physical being was anywhere even remotely close to me. The purpose of my questions or statements was to put any spirits in the theater at ease concerning our intentions.

As I was nearing the very back corner, I made the statement, "We can't see you, but you can see us." I was initially terrified when I received a response clearly stating, "Of course," in a very rough, gravelly voice that was coming from directly in front of me. It was as if a person were standing there conversing with me. I am being completely honest when I say the hairs on my arms and neck stood completely up, and I felt a shiver of fear course through by body. I waited a few seconds, and I shifted my feet on the wooden floor in an attempt to see if that was the noise I had heard, but my shoes didn't make any noise at all.

I then spoke my wife's name, and I am sure, had she been close enough to hear me, she would have heard the fear. I may have been a brave, hardened, and honed man, but I wanted out of that corner! While searching for the unknown, I found the unknown and then wanted away from the unknown. As I exited the stage area, I told everyone who could hear me about what I had experienced and I was sure I caught the EVP on tape.

Although many other exciting things happened to all five of us during the investigation, I couldn't get the EVP off my mind. When I got home, I listened to the recorder with amplified headphones on and the clarity of the words "Of course" absolutely amazed me. I had recorded the holy grail of EVP's on my very first hunt, an actual intelligent direct response to a question or statement. I saved the EVP on a disc and my computer, but I still have the original on the recorder.

Would you like to know what else took place during this "doing of something different"? I never thought about cancer once. I never felt any pain, even though at the time, my back was broken and a vertebra was slowly dissolving. I never focused on the fear of dying. I never worried about how people would get by without me. I was entirely caught up in the moment and the moment alone. I learned to chase my dreams and in the process found a peace that could only exist when my focus was shifted away from perceived problems and completely occupied by new experiences.

Since that time, I have been on many other ghost hunts, and I have a library of EVP recordings. The story as related above was the first time I felt the magic of traveling a different path, but it certainly wasn't the last. The most recent one I went on will not be the last one either, because my list of things I want to do continues to grow, plans continue to be made, and life goes on being experienced every day, hour, minute, and second I am here. My focus is on living, not dying.

While focusing on living, here are some of the things I do. I spend time loving my family. I have a wonderful circle of friends I spend time with. I fill my spirit with overflowing gratitude. I bicycle, kayak, go on short hikes, eat what I want to, go on vacations, go for walks, read books, go to football, basketball, and baseball games, go on weekend getaways, sleep in, arise early, sit and watch the sunset or witness the sunrise. I started a new hobby in photography. I keep a journal, write stories and a book, mow grass, ride the tractor, give tours of the stables, blog, and manage social media that applies to the business. I enjoy these and many other experiences that are way too numerous to list but can be summed up in two words: *I live!* I will as long as I possibly can, which with my mindset will be a long time yet.

When I started with life after the diagnosis, I spent too much time focused upon being tired, worrying about the future, and experiencing pain. Once I started doing the things I enjoy and the things I once thought were only dreams, my energy grew and feelings of hope coursed through my being. I allowed myself to become the most important person to me. I learned to say no without regret. I have even told doctors that treatments would have to wait until I was back from a road trip. Why? Because I am the most important factor in my happiness, and my happiness is required in order to allow my body, mind, and spirit to heal and grow.

I wonder if while reading this story you might be thinking I get a little confused sometimes concerning my belief system. I have written about energy healers, alternative therapy and treatments, Western medicine, meditation, guided meditation, environmental issues, and your body's natural ability to aid in healing itself. I have talked about near-death experiences, ghosts, quantum physics, mediums, psychics, positive thinking, belonging in a world made up of one's energy, a lack of belief in coincidence, and God. I have bragged about the power of proper, healthful nutrition and its ability to help your body slowly lower the level of harmful chemicals in the overflowing glass representing your being. I didn't go into the beliefs in rocks and crystals, which might have healing properties, nor did I mention the energy you can borrow from trees that are grounded to the earth even though I believe in both. I explained about the Law of Attraction, which many spiritual and very educated people believe is possible. I didn't speak of shamans or the wearing of a talisman to ward off disease or the great many other spiritual beliefs existing in this sphere we call home. Which of these do I believe? I believe all of them. I think the possibilities are absolutely endless, and you need to find what works for you and have one hundred percent faith in what you choose.

When I look back upon my life, it is no wonder I was diagnosed with a disease. At times in my life, I smoked, drank to excess, ate to excess, and ingested chemicals harmful to my body. I poured chemicals on my body and allowed them to be absorbed. I took prescription drugs that ended up being harmful. I carried the weight of regret and failed to forgive my own human nature. I unknowingly was subjected to drugs and chemicals in the food chain just because the FDA said the levels were safe for human consumption. I have drunk and bathed in water laced with fluoride and chlorine because, once again, science said the levels were safe. Now, there is other science saying they are not safe. Is it any wonder my glass filled up to over-flowing? I don't think so. So if I live the rest of my life believing in all of the subjects listed above and practicing good nutrition and safe hygiene, I am bound to live longer than I would if I continued to live as I had in the past and let the glass overflow. So yes, I believe in the possibility that all of the ideologies I listed above could individually or in combination be the magic we seek.

Of this much I am absolutely positive. There is way too much evidence available to discount the belief that death is a transition and nothing more. I told you early on in the story I do not have the answer to what happens to us when we die; I wish I did. But there is something else after death. There is much more to experience, and in time you will remember you have done this before.

In the center of my refrigerator, posted for me to see every morning when I awake and start the coffee brewing, is the following proverb: "Just when the caterpillar thought the world was over, it became a butterfly." And my belief is, so shall you, so shall you. The death of your physical shell will free your soul to emerge like the butterfly and transition to something new once again.

Chapter Seven

Lessons I Have Learned

IN THIS FINAL CHAPTER, I wanted to relay some of the lessons I have learned throughout my experience with this process. I don't think it would be possible for me to list everything I have learned, but I do want to share with you what I feel are some of the more important lessons.

I learned the elderly woman at the farmer's market who I previously mentioned was right when she said doctors don't always know what they are talking about. Let me be clear here and say there are a vast number of great Western medical doctors, and I do not mean to demean the profession. However, the first two we talked to regarding my diagnosis did not know what they were talking about, and one of them was a specialist in the disease. I did not become bed ridden within three months, and it has been over five years and I am still doing the things I want to do with a hale and hearty appetite for life.

My research tells me there are many people who live for years after being diagnosed with multiple myeloma. Some people live ten to fifteen years or longer. There is a bell curve applicable to longevity with this disease. Granted, a great number of the people with multiple myeloma will live three years or less, but there are just as many others who will live a much longer time. Maybe the ones who live the shortest amount of time listened to a doctor who drained all of the hope from them instead of looking for someone else who would instill in them a belief in miracles along with a healthy dose of optimism.

I learned a strong belief and faith in the ability to experience a cure goes a long way in the healing process. They also go a long way in life in general. Your desires and your dreams, when put in the proper context, are your power for growth and healing. I am reminded of a saying that was brought to my attention by an acquaintance. She was speaking about children when she said, "Children rise or fall to the level of expectations you have for them." In other words, you create the climate in your mind where opportunity is born.

When she said this, the light bulb in my mind became intensely bright. I believe her statement applies to all people, especially you. The expectations you have concerning yourself become your reality. How many people have you known or heard about who were told by a medical professional they had six months to live and then they died in six months? I certainly know of some situations where this was the case. It doesn't matter the amount of time a doctor might give you; what matters is they have planted the seed. It is important you do not tend the seedling. Doctors do not have a crystal ball to gaze into and tell you such things, and they shouldn't make a habit of doing so. It takes your hope away; believe me, I experienced it. They cannot look on your body and find a tag with an expiration date stating how long you will be in this realm of existence. They do not have a direct line to the Creator of this wonderful universe where they can call to inquire about your death date. Please do not let people steal your hope and faith. Run from anyone who tries to do this as fast as you can. Find someone who wants to help you emotionally and physically, not someone who wants to watch you fade away while making you comfortable.

While on the subject of the medical field, let me add another lesson I learned. Research completely any so-called maintenance drug prescribed to you by a medical professional before the first pill is swallowed and allowed into your system. As the name suggests, maintenance drugs are known as drugs you take on a regular basis for a long period of time, possibly the rest of your life. Would you take them willingly with the knowledge they may shorten life? Regardless of what the FDA, AMA, or anyone else tries to assure me to the contrary, I am convinced a steady diet of maintenance drugs led to the diagnosis I received. I believe that the consumption of the medications weakened my body to the point where disease was able to find a foothold.

Part of the proof of my beliefs is found in the evidence of how well I began to feel after discontinuing the drugs. Yes, they do studies, and they know the possible side effects related to certain medication, but they do not know enough about how these drugs interrelate when taken together. There is not enough evidence available to cause me to change my mind or my beliefs. Mainstream medicine knows this, yet doctors continue to write prescriptions for numerous medications to be taken at the same time without knowing the long-term possible effects of the combination.

On another note paralleling the subject of maintenance drugs, why don't scientists spend more time researching the placebo effect? From MedicineNet.com's MedTerm Dictionary, a placebo effect is "a remarkable phenomenon in which a placebo—a fake treatment, an inactive substance like sugar, distilled water, or saline solution—can sometimes improve a patient's condition simply because the person has the expectation it will be helpful . . . The more a person believes they are going to benefit from a treatment, the more likely it is they will experience a benefit." Placebos are used in drug trials to test the effectiveness of a new medication. Some people experience relief from the symptoms or outright cures, even if they did not receive the prescription drug. I believe more research needs to be directed toward this effect instead of creating new drugs.

The problem is, pharmaceutical companies cannot make money if the healing is accomplished by your mind, so they will not study the placebo effect. You have the same power to heal yourself that is evidenced with the placebo effect if you have complete faith in the method you are using. Your faith must be complete and unwavering.

I have learned you get back what you give. It does not matter if you give money, kindness, love, and time, or the negatives of fear, hate, anger, disappointment, or annoyance. You truly do get what you give. I have noticed it more so the past five years as it relates to what I give emotionally, but I have also known it to be the case with money for years. The more money I give to worthy causes, the more I do for people in need, the more of those things come back to me. It happens all the time, and it happens every time.

After experiencing it concerning money, my mind was opened to the possibility of it happening with other things. The kinder I am to people, the kinder people are to me. I have also found I attract people to me who have the same belief base that I have. I am surrounded with kind, loving, supportive, spiritual people who believe in magic and miracles. This just happens to be the perfect healing environment for me. I believe to get back what you give, you have to give without expectation of ever receiving anything in return. Give from the heart entirely for the good feeling giving grants you.

I have learned not to allow negatives I am faced with, whether big or small, to bother me at the level they once did. I used to be one of those people who would fly into a tirade when I or someone else made a mistake. I would feel put-upon if the misdeed came from someone else and angry at myself if I did something silly. I was especially bad when driving. No one's driving was on a par with mine. I would find fault with someone driving too slow, too fast, not signaling, pulling out in front of me, or doing anything else I judged to be an affront. I can proudly say I am now much more accepting of mistakes others or I make.

Who knows, maybe they aren't really mistakes! I had a thought one day early in the process of dealing with my reaction to negative events. What if the person you are behind, who is driving so slowly, is there for a purpose? Maybe they are protecting you. Maybe farther down the road someone is about to sneeze and drift into the oncoming lane and maybe, because you were forced to slow down and hadn't arrived at that spot yet, there will not be an accident. The possibility exists you are being held up for a reason. What if the person who just cut you off, or who just turned left in front of you, or who is daydreaming at a green light has their own burden to bear? What if they have just received the news they have cancer, or that a loved one does, or their beloved pet is missing, and they do not have their mind completely on what they are doing? What if their family is in turmoil because of misunderstandings? Would you be more forgiving if those were the circumstances? I know I would. Look beyond what you think you know to what else might be possible before you jump to conclusions. Be more forgiving of yourself and others.

I have learned meditation is an important tool to use when working on healing of your mind and body. It was one of the hardest things I have ever tried to master because to do it successfully, you need to quiet your mind. I bought books and videos and talked to others who have become good at the art and finally arrived at the point where I could go deep within myself. You do not have to have a subject matter to meditate; sometimes it is just a very deep, relaxed state of mind. There are times when I am doing a guided meditation I envision my body and being working on the cellular level to improve my health. I see white cells corralling cells that would harm me. I see red blood cells increasing in number to give me more energy. I see my lungs working perfectly and removing particles I have breathed into my system. I see my liver filtering just as it should in order to be healthier. Talk to your body silently about ridding itself of harmful toxins and rejuvenating your health.

I also find meditation is the key to good sleep. Your body needs rest in order to work optimally, and sleep is the key. If you can simply quiet your mind through meditative practices, you will sleep better, awake more refreshed, and feel healthier throughout the day.

I begin my meditative sessions with a relaxation phase. I slowly walk myself down several flights of stairs until I reach another world, a world of my creation. It has a country setting complete with an old red barn, the smell of freshly cut hay, and my old dog Sarge. All of these things are vividly seen and felt by my mind's eye. Growing up in the country and spending so much of my life with animals led me to create this place in my mind.

I have a great affinity for old barns. I feel they stand as sentinels to a long ago past and guard that past from an ever-changing way of life. They are not sleek and glamorous like the metal barns of today, but they have much more character in their aging beauty. They smell of the earth and the animals they protected from the elements while showing off the craftsmanship of prior generations. They stand as a doorway to our history. Simply said, they are a comfortable place to find peace. I think my description of old barns relates directly to the way I feel about my aging body. Those of us carrying the weight of years are no longer sleek like young people, but we have character in abundance lying in the folds of every earned wrinkle.

My advice to you is to use meditation to relax and heal. Find your personal place of peace, created by you for you alone, and visit it often. The end result will be a greater feeling of peace and contentment as well as more sound sleep. My wish for you, dear reader, and myself is that we will sleep with dreams of lightning bug hunts and campfire tales, back when life was simple and sleep was sure. Meditation will help you get there; just shut your eyes, quiet your mind, and look inside. Mahatma Gandhi said, "In the attitude of silence, the soul finds the path in a cleaner light and what is elusive and deceptive resolves itself into crystal clearness." Get past any negative perception of meditation you may have had in the past and try it; you may just find answers and peace.

I have learned to live in the "now" as much as possible, with the intention of getting ever better at it. This concept may seem a little strange at first, but believe me, it grows on you. To quote from *The*

Power of Now by the wonderful spiritual author Eckhart Tolle, "Life is now. There was never a time when your life was not now, nor will there ever be." The basic premise is that you need to try to focus your life and your appreciation for it on this very moment of your time of existence. It doesn't matter what you are focused on. It could be it a flower petal, the wind, a cloud, a loved one's voice, or any of the things you are experiencing at this moment; just focus on it completely. The message I get from this concept is to stop living in the past or attempting to live in the future. Be thankful for this very nanosecond you have been blessed with and experience it totally.

This is also a good way to start a meditation session. It clears your mind and makes your worries seem distant or nonexistent. It allows your focus to be on something completely separate from disease or uncertainties. Try it now. If you have a flower or a houseplant, look at it as if seeing it for the first time. Really take time to focus on the texture, varying colors, shape, and fragrance, and experience those things in the most minuscule detail, even down to any dust particles on the leaves. Keep doing it until you have had a complete experience before moving on. Living in the now helps you let go of past demons and future fears. It makes you appreciate what you have and that you have this time, right now, and only now.

The next lesson I learned was one of the hardest to grasp because it ended up being a complete change for me. You do not have to be everything to everybody. You do not have to fix everything that is broken, including relationships. You are allowed to say no when asked to do something. These things go together, and while admittedly difficult to master after a lifetime of doing all of them to excess, it became the most liberating of all the lessons I learned.

I have always been the go-to guy for almost everything. I was the one you could depend on to do a job, fix something broken, take on another responsibility, clean this, be there, act interested and supportive, and generally always say yes no matter that inside I wanted to scream a very loud *no*. I wonder if silently holding in resentment plays a part in making you more susceptible to disease. When you practice life as I did, you are putting the most important person in your life entirely at the end of the line in importance. The lesson was, I needed to be at the front of the line in order to be there for everyone else.

Love yourself first! That is not to say you need to be rude when you deliver a denial. Nothing impresses anyone more than a timely, sincere smile when you tell them you cannot do what they want you to do. You can still be kind and say no at the same time. Remember to put yourself at the front of the line in importance and you will find all of your relationships improving, especially the relationship you have with yourself.

I have learned there is a broad spectrum of support possibilities that accompany an end-of-life diagnosis when it comes to your family and friends. They range from completely supportive regarding the changes you are experiencing with a wonderfully positive and understanding attitude, to sudden and total abandonment at a time you need or desire their support and continuing love. Please try to remember, people operate from a position of fear or love and the people living on the negative side of this spectrum are operating from a place of fear. If they happen to be your mate, they may be very fearful of a future without you. If it is close friends or family, they may fear their own mortality and not want to face it through your experience. Regardless of their relationship with you, they may distance themselves from you in small steps now in order to lessen the pain when you do transition. It may be subconscious or it may be obviously intentional. Regardless of the emotional hurt, the only thing you can control if facing a rejection of this nature is your reaction to the perceived affront. Place your focus on the positive people in your life and forgive the negatives. Unfortunately, no matter how much you need things to stay the same regarding relationships, you might not be able to influence the coming changes in others. Although I am living closer to the positive end of this spectrum, I have witnessed those on the negative end. Remember, change is constant, lessons are abundant and in the end, all will be good.

I learned ridding the body of toxins regularly is a very important key to your longevity. There are many tools available which can assist you in giving toxins their eviction notice. Even if you eat organic, filter your water, and take all of the steps I have listed in this book concerning a healthier lifestyle, you cannot completely stop yourself from ingesting, breathing, or absorbing toxins unless you live in a sterile bubble, and I am not sure even that would work absolutely.

You must realize that as we walk through this world, we breathe air laced with particles having no business in our lungs. We find ourselves in places where we have to drink water or something else we have not filtered at home. These liquids have pollutants in them which are harmful. We touch plastics, solid surfaces, and other objects which give off chemicals or have been cleaned with products that give off chemicals, which are absorbed into our bodies. Even though the FDA approves these chemicals as safe for human consumption or contact by themselves, they know or publish little about what possible effects the combinations of these substances have on a human's body on a daily basis. It is much like the effects of maintenance prescription drug combinations; they don't know what the long-term effects will be on us. I have a feeling I do know and have experienced the effects.

I have learned not to care if the FDA and others listed in an alphabet soup of agencies say all these pollutants and chemicals exist in safe amounts for humans. I do not want them in or on me. I don't want you to become paranoid about life; I want you to go through it with the knowledge that these harmful things exist. Find ways to expel them before they have a chance to set up residence and harm you.

There are many ways to do this. I will list two, but before trying either, please get the advice of a naturopath or a holistic nutritionist. They can give you sage advice on how to proceed and will also watch over your progress. Fasting is one method which can be used once a week under the care of a professional. I use a liquid fast, where I drink juices and water one day a week. Another method is to do a periodic detoxification program. Make sure you have advice on this. It is a homeopathic regime which flushes toxins from your body.

There is also a method for ridding yourself of toxins that was developed by Edgar Cayce, whom I wrote about earlier. Mr. Cayce encouraged people to place a castor-oil-soaked piece of undyed flannel on the skin over the liver. You then cover the flannel with a piece of plastic and a heating pad and leave it for forty-five minutes or so to rid the liver of toxins. Castor oil packs can also be used on muscle aches and pains. I also learned through Mr. Cayce's writings about using castor oil on cuts, scrapes, and ingrown toenails in order to heal them. I am here to tell you it works—and works rapidly.

You can find all the data on castor oil packs at the Edgar Cayce Foundation Medical Research Division, Association of Research and Enlightenment in New York, New York. As you might suspect, these methods are not FDA approved, but what is important is they work! I find hot Epsom salt soaks in the bathtub are also useful for ridding the body of toxins, and as an added benefit, there are few things more relaxing than a hot tub and a good book.

Lastly, I will recommend my personal favorite, massage. I go once a week for a one-hour therapeutic massage by a licensed and trained massage therapist. Massage not only relaxes you and eases pain, but it also flushes toxins stored in the muscles of your body.

I learned every pain you experience is not cancer. It is funny, but prior to receiving the diagnosis I was gifted with, I often experienced pain of some sort in some part of my body, just as I imagine you do. It might have had a headache, indigestion, muscle pain and stiffness, a twitch here or a tweak there. I would guess you have gone through life in this way as well. It is common to feel some sort of pain every day. Before the diagnosis, I would never have thought of pain as anything more than just a discomfort caused by something I had done. However, after the diagnosis, I found myself wondering if a headache was a cancerous tumor in my brain or if a pain in my leg was a bone tumor. I wondered if a sore on my arm was a melanoma.

Everything I felt physically carried the possibility of being a related continuation of the diagnosis I lived with daily. Finally, sanity prevailed. I had pain before the diagnosis, and I would have pain afterwards. Pain could be just pain, like it was before I started living in a partly cloudy world, and not evidence of something more serious. Don't let your thoughts be guided or motivated by fear. Strive to find some sense of normalcy every day, because your soul is carrying a human body around, and it is normal to experience some discomfort during your travels. Perspective changes everything.

I have learned to become comfortable in the shell my soul carries around, regardless of how it has changed over the years. My body has a history, my history, written all over it. Consider this analogy. One day not long ago I was looking at an old horse saddle that was way past its prime. The thought occurred to me that I should get rid of it, but while looking at it, I realized this saddle might look old and worn out, but it too had a history. It had dependably traveled numerous miles and had seen a lot of places. It had been out in all kinds of weather and faithfully carried its owner without fail. Yet its soft leather seat was still as comfortable as always, if not more so. Its stitching and leather were still sound, even though showing evidence of repair. It other words, it might not look so good, but it was still serviceable. I realized my body and this old saddle had a lot in common. We might not look as good as we once did, but we were still useful and, I might add, comfortable!

I held one lesson I learned until the end of this book was drawing near. Throughout both parts of this book, you have read the words, "Things are what they are," or "It is what it is," or "Things are as they are supposed to be," or "What has happened was supposed to happen." Let me clarify something for you, because I believe it to be important. When things are as they are, it is an opening in your life for growth and change. You cannot look upon negative things occurring in your life as an ending; they are a beginning. They are a chance to change your outlook concerning how you plan to spend the rest of your life.

Acceptance of a fact does not mean accepting defeat. Accepting the fact I had received a diagnosis of a blood cancer did not mean I was going to lie down and die for anyone. Acceptance brought with it the chance for growth that changed my whole view of this life we lead. Now things for me are what they are supposed to be. I grew just as I was supposed to grow. I experienced a completely new view of my existence, and I believe what I found to be absolutely astounding.

Lastly, I have learned the death of the physical body should be a time of celebration and not one of sadness for those left behind. Don't be confused. I am not ready to die. I like the life I lead and the people I am surrounded by. I am not in any rush to leave this wonderful life I have been living. But when my time has come, I want people to celebrate the life I had instead of spending time crying over my absence.

Earlier in this book, I told of being angry with the Creator and asking him how he could dare to let me die when I have so much more to do. Well, a life lived right means you will never run out of things you want to experience, goals you want to reach, and things you want to see, so in my way of seeing things, it may never be a good day to die. Nevertheless, I know I am going to die, and I know you will too. Live on knowing I am convinced I will see you once again and may even be around in the shadows in the interim. I still don't have all the answers, but I am convinced death is not the end.

When the time comes that my physical body dies, I have asked my family not to have a funeral complete with depressing hymns and somber people crying in their tissues. Instead, I want them to set the stereo up at the horse barn, put on some sixties music, buy a couple of kegs of beer, invite whoever wants to come to the farm to celebrate my travels, sit around and tell stories of things I did while I was here, tell a few lies, laugh a lot, maybe cry a little, but mostly rejoice in the way

I exited. Have my physical remains cremated, burying part of me in a veteran's cemetery in Kentucky, my longtime home. Scatter the rest of my ashes in the ocean off the coast of Maine, where visits brought peace, quiet, and a time for introspection. The coast of Maine has a unique beauty that is forever etched in my very being and will be a good place to rest.

I hope I have brought peace to those who, like me, carry a life-ending diagnosis. I hope I have lightened your emotional burden in some way. When I started this book, one of my main goals was to bring hope to those who need something to lean on and to share my fervent belief in the great probability that life really does go on in some form or another after our human bodies cease to exist. I pray I reached that goal. Until we meet again, smile a lot, be at peace, and remember, I believe.

The end is never the end but instead
a place for pause before beginning
once again.

—Richard D. Rowland

Suggested Reading List

Alexander, Eben. *Proof of Heaven: A Neurosurgeon's Journey into the Afterlife.* Simon & Schuster, New York, 2012.

Altea, Rosemary. *The Eagle and the Rose: A Remarkable True Story.* Warner Books, New York, 1995.

Byrne, Rhonda. *The Secret.* Atria Books, New York, 2006.

Dyer, Wayne W. *There's A Spiritual Solution to Every Problem.* HarperCollins, New York, 2001.

Dyer, Wayne W. *The Shift.* Hay House, New York, 2010.

Gibson, Fred. *Old Yeller.* Harper & Row, New York, 1957.

McGarey, William A. *The Edgar Cayce Remedies.* Bantam Books, New York, 1983.

Myss, Caroline. *Anatomy of the Spirit.* Crown Publishers, New York, 1996.

Myss, Caroline. *Defy Gravity: Healing Beyond the Bounds of Reason.* Hay House, New York, 2009

Schwartz, Gary E., with William L. Simon. *The Energy Healing Experiments.* Atria, New York, 2007.

Siegel, Bernie S. *Love, Medicine, and Miracles.* HarperCollins, New York, 1986.

Taylor, Eldon. *What Does That Mean?* Hay House, New York, 2010.

Van Lommel, Pim. *Consciousness Beyond Life: The Science of Near-Death Experience.* HarperOne, New York, 2007.

Walsh, Neale Donald. *Conversations with God: An Uncommon Dialogue.* G.P. Putman's Sons, New York, 1996.

Walsh, Neale Donald. *Conversations with God: Living in the World with Honesty, Courage, and Love.* Hampton Roads, Charlottesville, VA, 1997.

Weiss, Brian. *Many Lives, Many Masters.* Simon & Schuster, New York, 1988.

Weiss, Brian. *Messages from the Masters.* Simon & Schuster, New York, 2000.

References

Bach, Richard. *Jonathan Livingston Seagull.* New York: Macmillan, 1970. Print.

Buffett, Jimmy. "Breathe In, Breathe Out, Move On." *Take the Weather with You.* RCA, 2006. CD.

Buffett, Jimmy. "Growing Older but Not Up." *Coconut Telegraph.* MCA, 1980. Vinyl.

Miller, Cheryl. "Peanut." Message to the author. 20 Sep. 2011. E-mail.

Miller, Cheryl. "Big News." Message to the author. 29 Sep. 2011. E-mail.

"Placebo." MedTerm Dictionary. Online, 1996-2012. Web. 2 Dec. 2012.

Puckett, Katie. "Katie's Kate Story." Message to the author. 29 Nov. 2012. E-mail.

Siegel, Bernie S. *Love, Medicine, and Miracles.* New York: Harper, 1986. Print.

"Serendipitous" and "Synchronicity." *The American Heritage Dictionary of the English Language.* Online, 2011. Web. 8 Dec. 2011.

Taylor, Eldon. *What Does That Mean?: Exploring Mind, Meaning, and Mysteries.* New York: Hay House, 2010. Print.

The Eagles. "Learn to be Still." *Hell Freezes Over.* Geffen Records, 1994. DVD.

Tolle, Eckhart. *The Power of Now.* Inner Growth Info. Web. 23 Oct. 2011.

Walsh, Neale Donald. *Conversations with God: An Uncommon Dialogue.* New York: G.P.Putnam's Sons, 1996. Print.